contemporary caribbean cooking

Sally Miller

acknowledgements

Firstly thanks to Goldie and David Speiler of Earthworks Pottery in Barbados, who gave me the run of their wonderful pottery and use of any and all of their whimsical functional pottery. My heartfelt thanks to all the people who generously shared their culinary secrets with me, because to some extent it is sharing a part of themselves: my mother, Eleanor Parris, my assistants Donna Jackson, Casandra Mayers and my aunt, Audrey Thomas. Also to my friends and family who contributed advice and help: Joan Taylor, Christine Wilkie, Vanita Comissiong, Benny Kirk, Sue Thomas, Pam Brooker, Gladys Kirton, Sister Barbara, Audine Bancroft, Marie Gurley, Charmaine St. John, Tim Boyce, Mosie Wardle and many others from whom I have learnt. To Artie for a superb job on the photography. Most importantly I would like to thank my husband, Keith Miller, who gave me the recipe of how to publish a cookbook

Created and written by: Sally Miller
Photography: Artie
Food styling: Sally Miller
Design: 809 Design Associates Inc.
Illustrations: Neil Barnard

Published by: Miller Publishing Co. Ltd.,
Williams Industrial Park,
Edgehill,
St. Thomas, BARBADOS
Telephone (246) 421-6700
Fax: (246)421-6707
e-mail: sally@millerpublishing.net

ISBN 976-8079-75-4

Printed in Singapore

contents

foreword

This book features a wide range of tried and tested recipes for popular, wholesome, home-cooked Caribbean dishes. The methods have been written very precisely with full explanations that are easy for anyone to follow. A great deal of testing has been carried out to ensure that the recipes really work.

People in the Caribbean will rejoice in a cookbook featuring ingredients that are readily available throughout the region but this cookbook is not intended to be limited to the sole use of people resident in the islands. On the contrary, West Indians living abroad and all friends of the Caribbean should also be able to make these dishes, wherever in the world they live, since the vast majority of the ingredients required can now be purchased in most major supermarkets.

I hope that my recipes will inspire people to get into the kitchen and prepare a wonderful variety of good West Indian food regularly. Preparing good food for yourself and your family everyday is surely the best ticket to health and happiness and it really is quite easily done!

Happy Cooking

Sally

Measurements

Measuring with cups and spoons is an easy way to cook and this is the first measurement given in each recipe. For those who are in the habit of cooking with scales and measuring jugs, each ingredient is also given in metric and imperial amounts. For those willing to convert to the cup system, get yourself two sets of the measuring cups shown here. Its' useful to have a set for wet and then dry ingredients.

Equipment

I have tried to make cooking easy and quick. This book is different in that equipment is brought into play to make cooking simpler and easier. A lightweight food processor and a hand blender are a boon to any cook. A lightweight food processor that can be lifted in and out of the cupboard with one hand means that it is easy to use. All you need on a daily basis is the steel blade and bowl. The other attachments won't be needed very often. Rather than write a cookbook with more of the same cake recipes, I have written them using a food processor. This makes the cake as easy to make as the instant box variety.

Speed is what today's busy cooks need.

caribbean seasoning/basil pesto/garlic in olive oil

Caribbean Seasoning: This is a cornerstone of tasty Caribbean cooking. This wonderful timesaver is used to season fish, chicken, meats, dips, stocks and soups. It is available ready made throughout the region, however, the homemade version in this recipe is especially delicious.
Basil Pesto: Although basil is best known as an essential ingredient in Italian cuisine, it grows almost wild throughout the Caribbean, year round. Originally brought to Egypt from India 4000 years ago, its name comes from the Greek word vasilikos meaning 'royal'. In addition to its culinary prowess; it has long been credited with healing powers. There are many varieties, but the broader leaf is preferable for this pesto.

Caribbean Seasoning
6 oz/185g green topped spring onions
I head of garlic
I lb/500g (6-7 medium) Spanish onions
Handful fresh thyme
Handful fresh marjoram
Handful of fresh parsley
Handful fresh basil
I tablespoon curry
I tablespoon salt
I tablespoon celery salt
I tablespoon paprika
2 tablespoons fresh ground black pepper
1/2 teaspoon ground cloves
I very hot red pepper or 3 chili peppers
or 2 tablespoons of red pepper sauce
Optional:
Handful of fresh coriander (cilantro, chardon beni)
Handful of celery leaves
All purpose powdered seasonings
Cumin and turmeric

1. Chop up the spring onions.
2. Peel and chop the Spanish onions.
3. Peel all the garlic.
4. Pick the leaves off the stems of the thyme, marjoram and parsley.
5. Place all the ingredients into a food processor and process for about 5 minutes.
6. Store in the fridge in two 10oz/300ml or one 20oz/600ml glass jar.

Basil Pesto
4-5 cups loosely packed 3oz/90g broad fresh basil leaves
I 1/2 cups olive oil
1/4 cup 1oz/30g almonds
1/4 cup 1oz/30g sunflower seeds
3 cloves garlic
I teaspoon salt
3/4 cup 3oz/90g grated Parmesan cheese

Serving suggestions:
• Toss with hot cooked pasta, along with sautéed vegetables, chicken or shrimp.
• Mix with cream cheese and serve with crackers.
• Add to all tomato-based sauces such as Chicken Creole, Meat Sauce and Chili Shrimp.
• Use as a marinade for fish along with additional olive oil and freshly ground black pepper or pepper sauce.

1. Put all ingredients into a food processor for 3 minutes.
2. Store in the fridge in two 10oz/300ml or one 20oz/600ml glass jar. Pesto lasts for weeks in the fridge and also freezes well for extended periods.

Garlic in Olive Oil
I lb/500g garlic (7-9 heads of garlic)
1/2 cup olive oil

1. Peel garlic and place in a food processor along with olive oil.
2. Process until garlic is finely chopped.
3. Store in the fridge in two 10oz/300ml or one 20oz/600ml glass jar.

pepper sauces

Pepper Sauces: Caribbean pepper sauces, sparingly used, add the pungent taste of the Caribbean to almost anything. Pepper lovers just can't get enough of the stuff. In the 1950's fresh horseradish was widely grown in Barbados and was a main ingredient in Bajan yellow pepper sauce. However, as the sauce became a commercial product, this dynamic ingredient faded out. This is reintroduced into this recipe. As a substitute you may therefore like to add horseradish powder. A hunk of cheddar cheese, some crackers, and a little bowl of this yellow sauce make a perfect snack to serve with drinks.

Red Pepper Sauce
4oz/125g green topped spring onions
3/4lb/375g (4-5 medium) onions
12 very red, hot fresh peppers
6 cloves garlic
1/4 cup 1oz/30g salt
21/2cups vinegar

Green Pepper Sauce
All the ingredients in the red pepper sauce except use hot peppers that are still green instead of red
3 cups 2oz/60g fresh basil or coriander

Sauce Ti Malice
3/4lb/375g (10 small) onions
3 cloves garlic
1 red sweet pepper
4 very hot, red or green fresh peppers
6 cloves garlic
Juice of 2-3 limes
1 tablespoon olive oil
Salt and freshly ground black pepper
1 cup 7floz/215g tinned or fresh tomatoes, peeled and chopped

Yellow Pepper Sauce
4oz/125g green topped spring onions
4-5 medium onions
12 very hot fresh peppers (bonnet) or 24 chili peppers
1/2oz/15g fresh turmeric or 1 teaspoon powdered turmeric
2 tablespoons English hot mustard
1/4 cup 1oz/30g salt
21/2cups vinegar
6 cloves garlic
1lb/500g grated fresh horseradish root or 1 tablespoon horseradish powder (optional)
3 dozen peeled pearl onions (optional)

1. Wash, peel and coarsely chop the spring onion and onions. Remove the stems from the peppers and for a less hot pepper sauce, remove the seeds. Peel the garlic.
2. Place peppers, onions, garlic, salt and 1/2 cup vinegar in the food processor and process for a few minutes. Wrap a kitchen towel around the lid as some processors spew when a thin liquid is processed. This can be particularly hazardous when making pepper sauce. When processed, add 2 cups vinegar.
3. Store in clean bottles.
4. Pepper sauce lasts for months without refrigeration.

1. Peel and thinly slice onions. Peel and finely chop the garlic. Deseed the red sweet pepper and hot peppers and slice.
2. Sauté onions, garlic and peppers in oil and lime juice for 10 minutes.
3. Add tomatoes and seasoning. Simmer for 5 minutes.
4. Cool and chill overnight. Serve cold with hot pork, fish or chicken.

How to handle fresh hot peppers
Wear rubber gloves or use a knife and fork. Do not touch yourself, or anyone else, especially around the eyes. Avoid too much handling and wash your hands thoroughly with soap and water as you finish.

1. Wash, peel and coarsely chop the spring onion and onions. Remove the stems from the peppers and for a less hot pepper sauce, remove the seeds. Peel the garlic.
2. Place the onions, turmeric, mustard, salt, peppers, garlic and 1/2 cup vinegar in a food processor and process for a few minutes. When processing be careful to wrap a kitchen towel around the lid as some processors spew when a thin liquid is processed.
3. Add, 2 cups vinegar, the grated horseradish and whole pearl onions. optional)
4. Store in clean bottles.

Mayonnaise

2 tablespoons flour
1-2 tablespoons white sugar
1-2 tablespoons light brown sugar
2 tablespoons hot English mustard
1 1/2 teaspoons salt
2 eggs
14oz/440ml can evaporated milk
1/2 cup malt/cider vinegar
1/4 cup lemon juice
1 tablespoon butter/margarine

1. Place water in the double boiler and bring to the boil. Two 10oz/300ml bottles should be placed in a saucepan completely submerged in cold water, boiled for a few minutes and kept hot to bottle the hot mayonnaise.
2. Place the dry ingredients in a medium bowl and mix. Add the eggs, unbeaten, and stir with a wooden spoon.
3. Add the milk and stir to blend.
4. Very gradually add the vinegar and lemon juice.
5. When water is boiling in the bottom of the double boiler, pour the mayonnaise into the top saucepan and stir constantly until it thickens. This should take 5-10 minutes. Do not let it thicken too much as it thickens further when chilled. If you cease stirring during cooking, it tends to form lumps.
6. Take off the heat and beat in the butter.
7. Bottle hot and refrigerate when cool.

Caribbean French Dressing

Whisk together:
1/2 cup olive oil
2 tablespoons lime juice
1 tablespoon white vinegar
2 tablespoons Dijon mustard
1 tablespoon minced garlic
1/2 teaspoon salt
1/4 teaspoon red pepper sauce
2 tablespoons grated onion

Ginger Citrus Dressing

Whisk together:
1/2 cup canola oil
1 tablespoon sesame oil
1 tablespoon grated orange rind
2 tablespoons lime juice
2 tablespoons balsamic vinegar
1 teaspoon light brown sugar
1 tablespoon fresh ginger finely chopped
1 teaspoon soya sauce

Basil and Balsamic Dressing

Whisk together:
1/2 cup 4floz/125ml olive oil
1/4 cup 2floz/60ml balsamic vinegar
3 tablespoons cup finely chopped fresh basil
1 tablespoon garlic
1 teaspoon light brown sugar
1/2 teaspoon salt
Freshly ground black pepper

Sauce Marie Rose

Whisk together:
1/2 cup 4floz/125ml mayonnaise
2 tablespoons tomato ketchup
1 tablespoon fresh lime juice
Red Caribbean pepper sauce or Tobasco sauce to taste
1 teaspoon sugar

mango chutney/sweet cucumber & onion pickles

Mango Chutney: This wonderful mango chutney recipe can also be made with other under-ripe fruit such as paw-paw or tomato. The mango should be under-ripe enough to be very acid. It is delicious served with pate, cheese and of course curry.
Sweet Cucumber and Onion Pickles (Bread and Butter Pickles): This easy recipe renders enough pickles for your own personal use. If you want to make a larger batch for gifts or to use up a glutt of cucumbers, then multiply it by 4 per batch. Serve with cheese, spicy seafood salad, fish terrine, sandwiches or burgers.

Mango Chutney
Enough mangoes that when peeled and
diced gives 2 lbs (900g)
4 cups best malt vinegar
4 oz/112g salt
8 oz/225g raisins
1 lb/450g currants
2 lb/900g golden crystal sugar
4 oz/112g peeled green ginger
1 oz peeled garlic
1 oz red hot pepper
2 oz mustard seed

Sweet Cucumber and Onion Pickles
1lb/500g cucumbers, small and thin with
very small seeds
1/2lb/250g onions, pearl onions if possible
1 tablespoon salt
1/2 cup 4floz/125ml white vinegar
1 teaspoon celery seeds
1 tablespoon mustard seeds
1/2 cup 2oz/60g granulated or castor
sugar

1. Use mangoes that are full but not ripe. On the first day peel and cut off the fruit in long thin strips. Rub in all the salt and leave for 24 hours.
2. Throw away the water that has drained from the mangoes and put them on to boil until soft in 2 cups vinegar. Set aside to cool.
3. Put the other 2 cups of vinegar into a saucepan with the sugar, boil up well, removing any scum as it rises.
4. Deseed the hot peppers, roughly chop the ginger and garlic and place them in a food processor and finely chop.
5. Remove the vinegar and sugar from the heat and put the chopped ginger, pepper and garlic mixture and stir well to break up any lumps.

6. Add the mangoes, raisins, currants and mustard seed and mix thoroughly over the heat. Let it simmer slowly for about 20 minutes to thicken. Allow it to cool thoroughly before bottling.
8. Bottles should be placed in a saucepan completely submerged in cold water, boiled for a few minutes and cooled, to be sure they are perfectly clean. Allow the bottled chutney to age for a few days before serving.

Makes four 8floz/250ml bottles.

1. Wash and slice the cucumbers.
2. Peel and slice the onions.
3. Layer the cucumber and onion slices in a bowl, sprinkling in between with salt. Place a small plate on top and press down with something heavy such a large jar full of something. Set aside for a couple of hours.
4. Measure the vinegar, celery seeds, mustard seed and the sugar into a medium saucepan. Bring to the boil and add well drained cucumber and onions. Keep turning until golden.
5. Pour into a bowl and cool.
6. Bottle in very clean 8oz jars and refrigerate.

drinks

Drinks: Punch comes from the Indian word "panch" which means five. The five refers to the five ingredients of sour, sweet, strong, weak and spice. The poem for rum punch goes:- One of sour, two of sweet, three of strong and four of weak, a dash of bitters and a sprinkle of spice, served well chilled with plenty of ice. A virgin daiquiri is made without rum and is a healthy treat. A Bentley is how pink lemonade originated. Ti panche was originally called Petite Panche and is a superb drink from the French Caribbean. Lime juice is best when extracted with a lime squeezer that sqeezes the skin and extracts the pungent citrus oil.

Ti Panche
1/2 lime
1/2 measure of sugar syrup
(follow the directions for making this in the rum punch recipe)
1 measure of rum

Stir the vodka, passion fruit syrup and 1/2 cup crushed ice. Strain into a martini glass Add a few chips of ice and decorate with passion fruit seeds.

Rum Punch
1 measure of lime juice, freshly squeezed
2 measures of sugar syrup - see method
3 measures of dark Caribbean rum, the older, the better
4 measures of water
Dash of Angostura Bitters and freshly grated nutmeg

1. Place two measures of sugar in a saucepan with a little water and cook until the sugar has dissolved and add to the juice.
2. Add the rum and water. A good quality passion fruit juice can be used instead of water but reduce the syrup slightly.
3. Serve with plenty of ice, a dash of bitters and a grating of nutmeg.

Passiontini
1 measure of vodka
1/2 measure passion fruit syrup/sauce
(store bought or homemade from the recipe on page 132)
Crushed ice

1. Squeeze the lime and place the juice and the sqeezed lime in the glass.
2. Pour over the syrup.
3. Add the rum.
4. Fill the glass with ice, stir well and serve.

Banana Daiquiri
1 banana
1 measure of Caribbean rum
1 cup 8floz/250ml chipped ice
1 tablespoon lime juice
2 tablespoons light brown sugar

Place all the ingredients in a blender. Blend for about 3 minutes.

Bentley
1 measure of lime juice
1 measure of sugar syrup
Ice and water to fill 10oz/300ml tumbler
1 cherry
Angostura bitters

Mix the lime, syrup, water and ice. Top with a dash of Angostura bitters and a cherry.

Leche
1 10oz/300ml tin condensed milk
1 tin 10floz/300ml dark Caribbean rum
Angostura bitters to taste
Grated nutmeg
2 tins crushed ice

Mix in a blender and serve with ice cubes and garnish with grated nutmeg.

avocadocrabpawpaw

appetizers

ackee & salt fish

This is a delightful Jamaican dish that is commonly served with crackers. Though usually prepared for breakfast, it has also become a very popular appetizer. An ackee is a red pear-shaped fruit that ripens on its tree and bursts open to reveal 3 large jet-black seeds that are surrounded by a cream-coloured aril. It is this aril which is then harvested and cooked. Delicious even when only dashed with a sprinkle of salt and pepper, this is a very versatile fruit. Note also that the tinned ackee is just as great tasting as the fresh and much safer to use since green ackee is poisonous. Though bacon – which has a very strong flavour - is traditionally used in its preparation, one may choose to use a little olive oil instead.

1 teaspoon finely chopped garlic
4 oz /125g frozen or tinned boneless salt fish
1 tablespoon olive oil or 2 strips streaky bacon
1/4 cup/1 medium finely chopped onion
1 16oz/540ml tin ackee (2 cups ackee drained)
Stripped leaves from a sprig of fresh thyme or a little dried thyme
1/2 cup/2 medium tomatoes, chopped
1/4 fresh red pepper very finely chopped or a dash of red pepper sauce (optional)
Garnish: Fresh tomato and parsley

1. If using tinned salt fish you may like to give it a little rinse, especially if you are using bacon as it can be a little salty. If using frozen salt fish place the salt fish in 4 cups of water and soak. Pour off the first set of water and add 4 cups of fresh water for 1/2 hour. If the salt fish is still too salty, repeat a third time.
2. Heat the olive oil or if using bacon, cut it up and fry up over a medium heat until it starts to brown. Add the onions and fresh pepper and allow them to brown. Drain off some of the bacon fat if you need to. Add the garlic and salt fish and continue to sauté for a few minutes.
3. Pour in the drained ackee, tomato, hot pepper to taste and add the fresh thyme. Sauté over a medium heat, stirring gently so as to somewhat preserve the delicate form of the ackee while blending it with the salt fish.
4. Serve warm or at room temperature.

Serves 2-3 for breakfast or 4 as an appetizer.

 buljol

The food in Trinidad and Tobago is widely acclaimed to be some of the tastiest in the Caribbean. Small wonder when the population originates from Africa, India, China, France and Spain. Buljol is a 'Trini' dish served with bakes (a bread cooked by frying) for breakfast. Served with crackers it is very popular to eat while relaxing with a few drinks and making some " old talk". Buljol is also a great picnic dish.

2 4oz/125g tins of salt fish or 8oz/250g boned salt fish
2 tablespoons lime juice
1/4 cup/4 tablespoons of olive oil
2 tablespoons finely chopped garlic (add gradually to suit taste)
1/4 cup/4 tablespoons finely chopped green topped spring onions or 2 medium finely chopped white onions or half/half
1/4 cup/4 tablespoons fresh parsley finely chopped
1 tablespoon fresh thyme
1/2 fresh green red pepper or 2 teaspoons of red pepper sauce
1 medium cucumber, peeled, seeds removed and diced

2-3 tomatoes, deseeded and diced
1/2 to 1 avocado, depending on size, diced (optional)
1 small sweet pepper, diced (optional)
Garnish: chopped parsley

1. If using tinned salt fish this step may be omitted. If using frozen salt fish, soak it overnight. Place the salt fish in a saucepan with 4 cups of water. Bring to the boil for a few minutes, pour off the first set of water and bring it to the boil a second time in 4 cups of fresh water for 1/2 hour. Cool and shred the fish.
2. Put the cooked and shredded salt fish, lime juice, olive oil, garlic, parsley, fresh thyme and pepper or pepper sauce into a bowl and mix well. Mix in the tomato and cucumber. Lastly, mix in the avocado, being careful to keep its small cubes intact.
3. Can be served right away but improves when allowed to stand for a couple of hours in the fridge.

4. Garnish with chopped parsley.

Serves 6 as an appetizer or 10 as an hors d'oeuvre

salt fish cakes

This first fish cake recipe is the flour-based version served at elegant cocktail parties and rustic rum shops throughout the Caribbean, the latter being three or four times the size of the former. As health conscious as we are all trying to be, hot fish cakes passed around at a gathering go like smoke in the wind. They are also popular as a take-away item, with the tell-tale grease stains seeping through the little brown paper bags they are often sold in. The potato-based salt fish cake is served as a main course and goes well with dressed cucumber, tomato salad, (page 56) and lettuce served with Sauce Marie Rose (page 9) and Pepper Sauce (page8).

Flour-based version

1/2lb/250g boneless salt fish
1 small onion finely chopped
3 cloves garlic finely chopped
1 tablespoon pepper sauce (optional)
1 1/4 cups 6oz/185g flour
2 teaspoons baking powder
1 egg
1/2 cup 4floz/125ml milk
1/2 cup 4floz/125ml water
1oz/30g butter
1/4 cup/2-3 finely chopped spring onions
Sprigs thyme, parsley, marjoram picked
from the stems and finely chopped,
Freshly ground black pepper, white
pepper and salt to taste

1. Place the salt fish in a saucepan with 6 cups of water. Bring to the boil for a few minutes, pour off the first set of water and bring it to the boil a second time in a fresh 4 cups of water for 1/2 hour. Check the saltiness of the fish. It should be salty but not overly so. If it is you may need to boil it up a third time.
2. Shred the salt fish with your fingers or a fork.
3. Put all of the ingredients in a mixing bowl and stir vigorously until a thick batter is formed.
4. Deep fry teaspoonfuls over a medium heat, until golden brown. Avoid the out side of the fish cakes burning before the middle is well cooked by carefully monitoring the heat.
5. Drain on absorbent kitchen paper.

Spicy Seafood Sauce

Mix the following:
1/2 cup tomato ketchup
Pepper sauce to taste
1 tablespoon lime juice
2 tablespoons horseradish (optional)

6. Serve hot with Marie Rose Sauce (page 9), pepper sauce (page 8) or spicy seafood sauce (above).

Potato-based version

1/2lb/250g boneless salted fish
1 small onion finely chopped
3 cloves garlic finely chopped
1 tablespoon pepper sauce (optional)
1/4 cup 1oz/30g flour
1 egg
1/4 cup 2floz/60ml milk
1lb/500g potatoes
1oz/30g butter
1/4 cup/2-3 finely chopped spring onions
sprigs thyme, parsley, marjoram picked
from the stems and finely chopped.
Freshly ground black pepper, white
pepper and salt to taste
Oil for frying

1. Place the salt fish in a saucepan with 6 cups of water. Bring to the boil for a few minutes, pour off the first set of water and bring it to the boil a second time in a fresh 4 cups of water for 1/2 hour.
2. Peel, dice and boil the potatoes until soft. Drain and mash the potatoes.
3. Shred the salt fish.
4. Mix all the ingredients together thoroughly.
5. Shallow fry in flattened spoonfuls over a medium heat until brown.
6. Drain on absorbent kitchen paper and serve hot.

fish terrine/spicy green mango salsa

Fish Terrine: This terrine can be made with different types of fish or just one kind. If using two different colours of fish you can split the ingredients and layer the two colours of fish for a stripped effect. For a richer flavour add 1/4lb/125g of smoked salmon. The delicate flavour of this terrine maybe enjoyed on its own, or may be dramatically complemented by Spicy Green Mango Salsa.

Fish Terrine
1lb/500g fish (mahi-mahi, wahoo, snapper, salmon)
A bunch of fresh herbs or 1 teaspoon dried herbs
1 bay leaf
1 envelope of gelatin
1/2 cup 4floz/125ml fish stock made with 1/2 fish stock cube
2oz/60g butter
2oz/60g cream cheese

1 teaspoon of red pepper sauce or cayenne pepper
1/4 cup 2floz/60ml dry white wine (optional)
2 tablespoons fresh lime juice
Garnish: Fresh herbs and lime slices

Spicy Green Mango Salsa
2 cups 8oz/250g green mango, very finely chopped
1 medium sweet pepper finely chopped
2 teaspoons red pepper sauce or cayenne pepper
2 tablespoons lime juice
salt to taste
2 tablespoons onion finely minced
1 tablespoon garlic finely minced
2 tablespoons pepper jelly

1. Wash and dry the fish and cut up into large cubes.
2. Melt the butter in a medium frying pan. Add the herbs, fish, lime juice, fish stock, wine,(if you don't want to use white wine, increase the fish stock by 1/4 cup) pepper sauce or cayenne pepper, bay leaf and sauté for five or ten minutes (just until the fish is cooked through).
3. Mash the cream cheese with a fork.
4. Remove the fish from the butter mixture, add to the cream cheese and mash gently with a fork.
5. Soften the gelatin in a little cold water. Bring the fish stock back to the boil, strain off the stock and dissolve the gelatin in it. Reserve 1/4 cup for the glaze and mix the rest in with the fish and cream cheese.
6. If you plan to turn out the terrine from a small loaf tin or fish mold, put the reserved glaze liquid in the bottom along with any garnish and place in the freezer for a couple of minutes before filling with the terrine mixture. If you are serving the terrine directly from a dish, then place the terrine mixture in the dish first and place that in the freezer for a few minutes before pouring over the glaze and decorating. Place in the fridge to set.
7. Sets in 3-4 hours. It is best to make this recipe the day before serving.

Serving suggestions:
• Slice and arrange around a mound of lightly dressed mixed leaf lettuce, thinly sliced melba toast or crackers and salsa or pepper jelly. Dressing page 11.
• Serve it whole, with salsa and crackers.

1. Mix all the ingredients together in a small bowl. This is an occasion where one can add a variety of fresh herbs, spices and sauces to create a unique and hopefully delicious concoction.
2. Store in the fridge for up to two days until ready to serve.

# rum chicken liver paté

The basis to most patés is a high proprtion of fat but the stock and gelatine in this recipe makes a slightly lighter and very tasty paté. It does need to be kept chilled until just before serving. Perfect for serving with drinks or as an appetizer.

12oz/375g chicken livers
8oz/250g streaky bacon
1 medium onion roughly chopped
2-3 bay leaves
1 tablespoon freshly ground peppercorns (preferably multi-coloured)
2/3 cup 5floz/150ml chicken stock (A chicken stock cube dissolved in 2/3 cup of boiling water is fine if you don't have any homemade stock)
2 packages of Gelatin (2oz)
1/4 cup 2floz/60ml good quality aged dark rum
4oz/125g butter

Garnish: Sprigs of fresh thyme, whole peppercorns, small bay leaves
1/2 of chicken stock and gelatin mixture reserved from the recipe

1. Cut each slice of bacon in four pieces, which can be done easily by cutting through the whole pack and then breaking apart. Fry in a large frying pan for a few minutes.
2. If the chicken livers come with hearts, remove them, and wash and drain livers. Add livers, onions and bay leaves to bacon and continue sautéing on a medium to high heat, stirring periodically, until the livers are nicely browned, 10-15 minutes.
3. Still over the heat, remove the bay leaves and pour in the rum. Light the mixture carefully with a match and burn off the alcohol content, (flambé) (If you are nervous of doing this just add the rum and proceed without burning it).
4. Make up the chicken stock by dissolving the chicken cube in boiling water or bring 2/3 cup of chicken stock to the boil. Soften the gelatin in a 1/4 cup of water and dissolve in the hot chicken stock. If you prefer to turn out the paté, you can pour 1/2 of this stock and gelatine mixture into a well greased foil loaf tin, garnish with fresh thyme, bay leaf and mulit-coloured peppercorns and set quickly in the freezer. For extra safety, you can line the tin with cling film before pouring in the stock. This makes it very easy to turn out. Of course you can skip out this whole part and simply set your pate in a dish, topping it off with the glaze later.
5. Put the livers, 1/2 of the stock and gelatin mixture, the butter and the freshly ground black pepper into a food processor and process for a couple of minutes.
6. Pour mixture into one or several dishes, cover and chill in the freezer for a few minutes. Finish the top with the rest of the stock and gelatin mixture. Garnish and refrigerate.
7. Sets in about 4 hours. To speed up setting, place in a freezer for about 1/2 hour.

Serves 8 as an appetizer or 16 as an hors d'oeuvre.

Serving suggestions:
- Set in 8 ramekin dishes or two shallow dishes and serve with a basket of homemade melba toast or crackers and mango chutney (page 10)
- Set in a shallow 8" long rectangular dish or foil tin. Turn out and slice. Serve around a mound of lettuce, dressed in a light balsamic vinegar and olive oil dressing, interspersed with teaspoonfuls of mango chutney and slices of homemade melba toast or crackers.

pickled or soused conch/ceviche

Ceviche: This is delicious when served with crackers or just on its own as a fat-free starter. And though the idea of making it with really fresh fish is especially appealing, frozen fish is fine. Ceviche, by the way, is also renowned for its effectiveness in treating hangovers.

Pickled or Soused Conch: In the islands where conch is plentiful it is prepared in a variety of ways such as curry and stew but this is one of the nicest conch dishes served in the islands.

Pickled or Soused Conch
1/2lb/250g conch meat, cleaned and pounded
1/2 cup/1 medium onion, chopped
2 cups/3-5 cucumbers, finely chopped
1/2 cup/2 medium onions, finely chopped
1/3 cup lime juice (juice of 2 or 3 limes, enough to give the pickle a good twang)
1 teaspoon salt
Small bunch parsley, finely chopped
1 teaspoon hot pepper very finely chopped or 1/2 teaspoon red pepper sauce
1/4 cup/1 finely chopped sweet pepper (red or green)

1. Cook the conch in salted water until tender. A pressure cooker comes in handy for this process.
2. Meanwhile, prepare the pickle of cucumber, onion, lime juice, salt, parsley and hot pepper and refrigerate.
3. Cool and cut the conch into very small pieces. Leave to marinate in the pickle and refrigerate for at least 2 hours - the longer the better (overnight is best!!)
4. Serve with crackers.

Ceviche
1lb/500g fresh mahi-mahi, wahoo, barracuda, salmon or any firm fleshed fish.
1/4 cup 2floz/60ml fresh lime juice
1 teaspoon salt
1 tablespoon vodka (optional)
2 tablespoons olive oil
2 medium onions in wafer thin rings
A little hot pepper very finely chopped
Fresh parsley or coriander to garnish

1. Place the lime juice, salt, oil, hot pepper and vodka in a shallow container or zip lock freezer bag.
2. Slice the fish as thinly as possible. If you do use fresh fish, it is easier to cut wafer thin when you partly freeze it.
3. Alternate layers of the fish and the onion rings in the pickling liquid, making sure that all of the fish is thoroughly coated. Refrigerate, turning a couple of times over an hour.
4. Serve garnished with fresh parsley or coriander.

Serves 6

 wontons

These are always very popular. Once you can get hold of the wonton papers which many supermarkets now stock, they are very easy to make. They can be frozen separately on baking sheets and then stored in the freezer in zip lock bags. When you take them out of the freezer, place them on a baking sheet or platter before they thaw out and stick together. These wontons can also be steamed or added to a broth with vegetables and chicken to make wonton soup.

1lb/500g peeled shrimp, pork or
boneless chicken
1/4 cup 2floz/60ml soya sauce
Red Caribbean pepper sauce or Tabasco
to taste
1 tablespoon oil (sesame or spicy stir fry
oil are best)
1 small onion
2-3 green topped spring onions/scallions
Small tin 8oz/250g sliced water
chestnuts
Pinch Chinese five spice powder
1 egg

2 packages Wonton skins (35-40 skins)
1/4 cup 1oz/30g corn flour or
arrowroot flour
1/2 teaspoon white pepper
1 teaspoon sugar
3 cups 24floz/725ml oil for deep frying

1. Finely chop the shrimp, pork or chicken in a food processor for 10-20 seconds.
2. Marinate in soya sauce and pepper sauce.
3. Finely chop the onions, scallions, and water chestnuts.
4. Separate the egg and set aside.
5. Heat the oil and sauté the onions. After a couple of minutes add the pork, chicken or shrimp, water chestnuts, the egg yolk, white pepper, sugar and five spice powder and sauté until nicely browned.
6. Set aside to cool.
7. Place a teaspoonful of mixture in the centre of a wonton skin, fold over a corner and dab on top with egg white, fold the opposite corner over and dab on top of that with egg white, twist and press the two remaining corners in opposite directions onto the sticky centre. Place on a large pan or dish that

has been dusted with corn flour or arrowroot flour.
8. Heat the oil and deep fry over a medium to high heat for 30 seconds to a minute until light brown and crispy.
9. Serve with Soya sauce, sweet chilli sauce or spicy tamarind dip.

Makes about 35-40 wontons

sesame chicken wings

Popular with all ages, these are great to have with drinks, a buffet or as a starter. They work well for picnics or boat trips because they can be served at room temperature. Finger licking stuff!

2-4lbs/1-2kg chicken wings, depending on whether you serve the whole wing or just the meaty third

Marinade:
1 cup 8floz/250ml peanut oil
1/2 cup 4floz/125ml sesame oil
1 cup 8floz/250ml soya sauce
2 tablespoons pepper sauce or Tabasco
1/2 cup 4floz/125ml honey
1/2 cup 2oz/60g brown sugar
1/2 cup 2oz/60g sesame seeds

1. Mix up the marinade of peanut oil, sesame oil, soya sauce, pepper sauce, honey and brown sugar and set aside.
2. Wash and pick the chicken wings making sure all the feathers have been removed. You can either tuck in the third end of the wing like the photograph opposite, cut it off or cut off both of the thinner sections, using only the meaty third.
3. Place the chicken in a large shallow dish or a zip lock bag, pour over the marinade, making sure that all the wings are well coated. Leave to marinate overnight or for at least 4 hours.
4. Preheat a slow oven 325F, 160C or Gas Mark 3. Bake in a large enough pan that the wings are not touching very much, with 1/4 of the marinade and the sesame seeds for about 1/2 hour.

5. Baste and turn the wings a couple of times during baking to ensure that they are nicely browned all over, adding more of the marinade, if necessary, to keep them moist.

Serves 4 as a starter or 8 as an hors d'oeuvre

callaloo soup & split pea soup

Callaloo Soup: The recipe below allows one to use either plain water or stock made from cubes. Either will result in a tasty soup, as onions herbs and crab will be added in the process.

Split Pea Soup: This is the thing to cook when there is a left over ham bone. The mere mention of this dish and West Indians, especially men, sing about the virtues of their "big soup" which usually includes split peas and anything or everything that they can find.

Callaloo Soup

1/2lb/250g callaloo leaves (Dasheen),
fresh spinach can be substituted
3 tablespoons butter
1 medium onions finely chopped
1 teaspoon garlic finely chopped
6 cups 48floz/1.5l chicken stock or water
1/2lb/250g crab meat
1/2 cup 4floz/125ml coconut milk
(coconut milk powder is excellent for
this)
1/2–1 teaspoon salt depending on how
salty the stock is
1/4 fresh herb leaves, chopped (thyme,
margaram and chives)
Freshly ground black pepper
Red pepper sauce to taste

1. Wash the callaloo leaves under cold
   running water and discard any
   discoloured leaves. If using spinach,
   shred it into strips.
2. In a heavy saucepan, melt the butter
   over a medium heat and sauté the
   onions and garlic until soft.
3. Add the leaves and turn them for a few
   minutes until they are well coated in
   butter and limp. Add the stock/water,
   herbs, half of the crab, coconut milk, salt
   and pepper. Bring to the boil then
   reduce the heat and simmer for 20-30
   minutes. Add pepper sauce to taste.
4. Add the other half of the crab meat,
   simmer for a couple of minutes to heat
   the crab through and serve.

Split Pea Soup

5 cups 40floz/1.2l water
Sprigs of thyme, parsley and marjoram
Celery leaves or a stick of celery
1-2 whole, green topped spring onions
1 tablespoon black peppercorns
1 onion
1 chicken stock cube
Ham bone or 1/2lb/250g salt meat
Chicken bones or a chicken leg and thigh
(When you bake a chicken, save the
bones in your freezer to make soup)
1oz/30g butter
1lb/500g pumpkin or squash
1lb/500g split peas

1. Place the water, herbs, onion, freshly
   ground pepper, chicken stock cube,
   bones and salt meat in a saucepan.
   Bring to the boil and then simmer on a
   medium heat for an hour.
2. Strain the stock and return to the heat
   with the pumpkin, peeled and roughly
   chopped, split peas and butter.
3. Boil for 20-30 minutes or until the peas
   and pumpkin are well cooked.
4. Cool and blend until smooth in a
   blender. Add salt and pepper to taste.
5. Freeze if not serving immediately.
6. When ready to serve reheat over a
   medium/low heat.

Serves 4-6

gazpacho

The tomato was first encountered by the native populations of South America who introduced it to the Caribbean. When the returning Spanish conquistadors introduced it to the Europeans in the sixteenth century, it was the first time that the people of Spain and then Italy had ever seen a tomato - and the rest, as the say – is culinary history. As with most things tomatoes grow year-round in the Caribbean. Gazpacho, served throughout the Spanish Caribbean perfectly suits the climate.

1 large can 32floz/100ml tomatoes or
2lbs/1kg tomatoes, scalded and peeled
2 sticks celery
1 medium cucumber, peeled, with the
seeds removed
1/2 sweet pepper
1/2 medium onion
3 tablespoons finely chopped watercress
(optional)
2 tablespoons parsley
1/2 cup 4floz/125ml olive oil
1 tablespoon lime juice
1 clove garlic
1 teaspoon salt
1/2 teaspoon freshly ground pepper

3 dashes of red pepper sauce
1 8 floz/250ml tin of V8 or tomato juice
1/2 cup 4floz/125ml dry white wine
Garnish: Croutons, chopped fresh
parsley or basil sprigs.

Can be served with
Cucumber, diced
Celery, diced
Sweet pepper, diced
Avocado, sliced

1. Trim, wash and roughly chop all the
   vegetables.
2. Grind the first 13 ingredients, from the
   tomatoes to the red pepper sauce, in a
   blender. For a course Gazpacho just
   grind for 20 seconds, for a finer mix run
   for about 2 minutes.
3. Mix in the V8 or tomato juice and white
   wine.
4. Chill overnight.
5. Serve in bowls with three or four
   croutons and chopped parsley placed in
   the centre. For a more substantial
   gazpacho you can serve it with diced
   cucumber, sweet pepper, celery, and
   extra croutons.

The two main variaties of pumpkin found in the Caribbean are Garden and Belly. Belly pumpkin is more fibrous and most commonly used for soups. This soup is also delicious made with squash.

1lb/500g chicken with bones and skin or
left over baked chicken bones
5 cups 40floz/1.2L of water
Sprigs of thyme, parsley and marjoram
Celery leaves or a stick of celery
1-2 whole, green topped spring onions
1 tablespoon black peppercorns
1 onion
1 chicken stock cube
1oz/30g butter
3lbs/1.5kg Pumpkin

Garnish: Fresh cream, parsley or thyme

1. If using chicken, remove any fat, but not the skin since it gives the stock a good flavour.
2. Place all the ingredients except the pumpkin and the butter into a saucepan. Bring to the boil and then simmer on a medium heat for 1/2 hour.
3. Remove all the chicken and vegetables from the stock by pouring through a colander or strainer and return to the heat in the saucepan with the pumpkin peeled and roughly chopped. Boil for 1/2 hour or until the pumpkin is well cooked. If using chicken, either add the cooked chicken meat to the soup or use it otherwise.
4. Cool and mix in a blender and add salt and pepper to taste.
5. Freeze if not serving immediately.
6. When ready to serve, reheat over a medium heat.
7. Serve garnished with fresh parsley or a small blob of cream, dropped in the centre of each bowl and swirled gently with a pointed knife or toothpick.

Serves 4-6

shrimp, avocado and paw paw salad

Both avocados and paw paws are ripe when they form a dent when pressed with a finger.

2lbs/1kg raw medium to large shrimp with shell on or
1 1/2 lbs /750g shelled cooked shrimp
1 cup 8floz/250ml fresh milk
6 slices of streaky bacon
1 small ripe paw paw
1 large or 2 small avocado pears
6 small portions mixed leaf lettuce
2 tablespoons dried chilli flakes or red peppercorns

Sauce Marie Rose (page 9)
Ginger Citrus Dressing (page 9)

1. If the shrimp are raw, shell, slit open along the back and remove membrane. Marinate in 1 cup milk for 1/2 hour. Then poach the shrimp in salted water for 2-3 minutes depending on the size, drain and chill.
2. Fry the bacon until crispy over a medium low heat. Cool on absorbent paper and crumble. Set aside.
3. Cut the paw paw in quarters, remove the seeds, peel off the skin with a sharp knife and slice. Cut the avocado in quarters and remove the seed. Sometimes there is a thin skin in the centre of the pear around the seed which also must be peeled off. Pull off the outer skin of the avocado, which should come off easily if it is perfectly ripe, and slice.
4. Wash, dry and tear the lettuce leaves. Toss in a little ginger citrus dressing to lightly coat them and place in mounds in the centre of 6 plates.

5. Arrange the slices of avocado and paw paw along with the shrimp around the lettuce.
6. Sprinkle on the bacon and red peppercorns or chilli flakes.
7. Put squirts or spoonfuls of sauce marie rose on the plate. If you want to do an artistic pattern with sauce, put it into a plastic sauce dispenser with a nozzle like those commonly used for ketchup and mustard. Serve immediately.

Serves 6

spicy seafood salad

The taste of the hot pepper, sour lime, sweet brown sugar and salty fish sauce should be subtle and well proportioned in this salad. The idea is to enhance the flavours and textures of delicious Caribbean seafood.

1/2lb/250g cleaned shrimp
1/2lb/250g lobster tail meat
3oz/90g squid, sea cat or calamari, cleaned
1/4 cup 2floz/60ml lime juice
1 tablespoon red pepper sauce (adjust to taste)
2 tablespoons sugar
1/4 cup/4 tablespoons fish sauce
1 cup/ 6oz/185g red, yellow, green and/or orange sweet peppers, cut in thinnest possible slivers (julienne)
1/2 cup/1 medium purple onion, cut in wafer thin slivers

1/2 cup/handful loosely packed fresh coriander (cilantro, chardon beni)
Salt to taste
Garnish: pickled cucumber (page 10) and fresh coriander (cilantro, chardon beni)

1. Clean and cook all the seafood in salted water separately. The shrimp takes 2-4 minutes in boiling water depending on size. The lobster takes 5-15 minutes of boiling depending on the size of the tail or tails. The squid takes about 1/2 hour of simmering over a low to medium heat.
2. Cut the shrimp in half if they are large. Slice the lobster into medallions. Slice the squid into rings.
3. Mix up the lime juice, sugar, fish sauce and pepper sauce until the sugar is dissolved and add salt to taste.
4. Combine the seafood, peppers, onions, coriander and dressing and refrigerate for up to 12 hours.
5. Serve garnished with pickled cucumber and fresh coriander.

Serves 4-6

crab crepe

The good thing about these delicious crepes is they can be made ahead of time, refrigerated and then baked just before serving. The bad thing is that it takes a fairly long time to cook 6 crepes. If planning to use at a later date it is best to freeze the crepes between sheets of wax paper in an airtight bag or container.

Crepes

1 cup 8floz/250ml fresh milk
1 cup 8floz/250ml water
1 cup 5oz/155g flour
1 egg (depending on size)
1 tablespoon lime juice
1/2 teaspoon salt
Butter for frying

Sauce

1 1/2oz/45g butter
1/3 cup 2oz/60g cup flour
3 cups 24floz/725ml milk
8oz/250g cheddar cheese, grated
1/2 teaspoons onion grated or onion powder
1/4 teaspoon garlic grated or garlic powder
1/2 teaspoon hot English mustard powder or Dijon mustard forte
Salt and white pepper to taste

Filling

2 small tins or 12oz crab meat
1-2 teaspoons red pepper sauce or cayenne pepper
2 tablespoons chopped spring onions/scallions
1 teaspoon lime juice
Salt to taste
Garnish: finely chopped scallions and grated cheese

---

1. Blend all the ingredients for the crepes (A hand blender is perfect for this task but a wire whisk or regular blender will work).
2. Heat a knob of butter in 8"/20cm non-stick frying pan over medium heat and pour in 1/3 cup crepe batter, spreading well. Fry over a medium heat and ensure that the crepe is well cooked on both sides. Repeat until all 6 crepes are cooked. You should remove the pan from the heat, between crepes. This will prevent the pan from getting too hot You may also have to give the pan an occasional wipe with some absorbent paper to remove any little bits that will burn. Try not to leave the crepes unattended when cooking as they burn easily. There is enough batter for 7 crepes (one extra crepe).

1. Melt butter in a small saucepan, add flour and cook for a couple of minutes over a medium heat, stirring.
2. Gradually add the milk, removing from the heat and beating each time it reaches boiling point, to blend.
3. Add dashes of white pepper, garlic powder, onion powder and mustard. Stir until nicely thickened and add all the cheese. Cook on a medium heat for 3-5 minutes to melt cheese.
4. Taste and add a little salt to taste, if necessary.

1. Grease either six individual gratin dishes or one oblong dish and pour a little cheese sauce in the bottom.
2. Mix the crab, scallions, pepper, lime juice and add a little salt to taste. Add a little of the cheese sauce and divide into 6 portions. Fill each crepe with crab mixture and roll.
3. Place the rolled crepes in the dish, pouring the remaining cheese sauce on top in a pattern so as not to smother. Sprinkle with a little grated cheese.
4. Preheat the oven for 10 minutes at 350F, 180C or Gas Mark 4 and bake the crepes for 10-15 minutes or until light brown and bubbling.
5. Garnish with finely chopped scallions.

Serves 6

melongeneokrabreadfruit

vegetables & salads

okras creole/plantains wrapped in bacon

Okra: Also known as ochros or lady's fingers, tend to become very slimy when overcooked. In fact, the gummy sap that they lend to soups is where the word gumbo originated. The smaller okras, which are the most tender, boiled or sautéed for a short time, are firm and delicious. The recipe below has its roots in the Indian Cuisine of Trinidad and Tobago, and is best served as a side dish with fish or curry.
Plantains Wrapped in Bacon: This simple dish is as delicious as it is easy.

Okras Creole
15-20 small okras
1 tablespoon olive oil
2 tablespoons cumin seeds
2 medium onions finely chopped
1lb/500g tomatoes chopped
1 teaspoon turmeric powder
1/2 teaspoon chilli powder
Salt and pepper to taste
Garnish: Fresh coriander

1. Heat the oil in a medium saucepan or frying pan.
2. Sauté cumin seeds until they pop and the onions until they lightly brown.
3. Add the tomato, turmeric, chilli powder, salt and pepper on a medium heat for a couple of minutes.
4. Remove the stems and tops from the okras. If they are small, add them whole. If they are large, chop them into 1 1/2"/3cm pieces. Cover and reduce the heat to low, simmering for about 5 minutes. Be careful not to overcook. Garnish with fresh coriander.

Serves 4

Plantains Wrapped in Bacon
3 Ripe plantains
6oz/185g pack of streaky bacon

1. Preheat the oven to 350F 180C or Gas Mark 4.
2. Cut the pack of streaky bacon down the centre.
3. Peel the plantains and cut them into strips of 2"/5cm in length.
4. Wrap each piece of plantain in 1/2 a piece of streaky bacon.
5. Bake the plantains for 20-25 mins or until a nice colour brown.

Serves 6-8

Plantains are grown and eaten throughout the Caribbean. Masquerading themselves as very large bananas, these vegetables are unpalatable unless cooked, and can be prepared at all stages of ripeness, with stark contrasts of texture and flavour. When they are unripe, and as hard as potatoes, they may be peeled and boiled as a bland, starchy accompaniment to stews. Ripe, they can be baked whole in a medium oven for 15-20 minutes and served either in their skins or peeled and sliced. In Puerto Rico ripe plantain is sliced and rolled into rings, filled with a spicy ground beef mixture, and baked. But it is when plantains are over-ripe and speckled with black that they are best sliced diagonally and sautéed in a little shallow oil. It possesses a deniable but subtle sweetness that goes exceptionally well with chicken, pork, and fish.

fritters

Pumpkin Fritters: The creamier Garden Pumpkin is most commonly served boiled or in fritters while the slightly more fibrous Belly pumpkin is more suited to soups. Pumpkin fritters are served sprinkled with sugar and spice, but they are eaten as a side dish, not a dessert.

Eggplant Fritters: Eggplant (also referred to as aubergine, melongene, bolangere) grows very easily in the Caribbean and are therefore available year round at very reasonable prices. Once the bitterness is dealt with by marinating in salt, eggplant has a superb texture and taste.a

Pumpkin Fritters
2lbs/1kg pumpkin
Salt
3 tablespoons brown sugar
2 teaspoons mixed powdered spice or cinnamon
1 egg
1 cup 5oz/155g flour
2 tablespoons milk
2 teaspoons baking powder
Canola oil for frying
Garnish: 2 tablespoons brown sugar mixed with 1 teaspoon mixed powdered spice

Eggplant Fritters
1lb/500g eggplant
2 cups 16floz/500ml lightly salted water
1/2 cup 2oz/60g flour
1/2 cup 2oz/60g fine breadcrumbs
1/2-1 teaspoon salt
1/2 teaspoon white pepper
1/2 teaspoon garlic powder
1/2 teaspoon onion powder
1 teaspoon of general seasoning powder
2 eggs
Canola oil for frying

1. Peel, cut up and boil the pumpkin in salted water until soft.
2. Drain and mash pumpkin. In a little bowl mix the sugar and spice and add to the pumpkin.
3. Whisk an egg and mix into the pumpkin along with the milk. Add baking powder and flour until it comes to a good dropping consistency.
4. Shallow fry both sides on a medium heat until dark brown. Adjust heat when cooking so fritters cook through without burning. These fritters should be fairly thin with a creamy consistency inside when cooked.
5. Serve hot, sprinkled with the mixture of sugar and spice.

Makes 20-25 fritters.

1. Wash, peel and cut the eggplant and cut it into 1/2" thick slices, discarding the two ends. If you prefer you may leave on the eggplant skin. If the eggplant are large, cut each slice in half or quarters.
2. Place in a collander and cover in salt for 5 minutes, draining. This removes the bitter taste. Wash and drain.
3. Beat the egg.
4. Mix the flour, breadcrumbs and seasonings and place in a small shallow pan.
5. Coat each slice of eggplant in the egg, and then coat in the seasoned breadcrumbs. During this process, shake off any excess egg and breadcrumbs. Excess egg causes the fritters to burn easily and excess breadcrumbs tend to fall off during frying and burn in the oil, spoiling the flavour and appearance of the fritters.
6. Heat the oil and fry the fritters over a medium heat, turning so that they are brown on both sides.
7. Take off any excess oil by placing fritters on absorbent paper and then serve on a heated platter.

Makes 16-20 fritters.

Green String Beans & Sautéed Almonds: This is an effective way to cook beans without them losing their colour. If you are using tender little French beans, omit slicing them lengthways.

Glazed Carrots: This recipe seeks to enhance rather than overpower the sweetness of carrots and preserve their vitamins and flavour by cooking them in their own juices rather than water.

Green String Beans & Sautéed Almonds

3/4lb/375g green string/french beans
Salt
1 tablespoon butter
1/2 cup 2oz/60g sliced almonds

1. Top and tail, wash and slice the green beans lengthways.
2. Cook until just tender in salted boiling water, (3-5 minutes, depending on thickness) being careful not to overcook.
3. Drain and set aside.
4. When ready to serve, melt the butter in a frying pan and sauté the almonds until just beginning to turn golden. Add the cooked beans, toss in the almonds and butter until hot and serve.

Glazed Carrots

1lb/500g carrots
2 tablespoons butter
Freshly ground black pepper
1-2 teaspoons sugar to taste
1/2 teaspoon salt

1. Peel, top and tail and wash the carrots. Cut them up into circles 1/2" thick or sticks. If they are very small, leave them whole.
2. Place all the ingredients into a small saucepan on a medium heat. Once the butter has melted, cover tightly and reduce the heat to low.
3. Cook for 5-8 minutes until the carrots are cooked but still al dente or slightly crunchy.

christophene au gratin/vegetables in cheese sauce

Christophene Au Gratin: Also known as chocho, christophene is a small, sugar free member of the melon family. Though most often cooked, it is also delicious when just peeled, cored, thinly sliced and eaten raw with a little vinaigrette.

Vegetables in Cheese Sauce: This is a great way to get picky eaters, especially children, to eat healthy vegetables. And one may choose to use just one vegetable such as cauliflower or the variety in the below recipe.

Christophene Au Gratin
4 christophenes
2oz/60g butter
1/4 cup/4 tablespoons flour
1 1/2 cups 12floz/360ml milk
12oz/375g cheddar cheese, grated
1 teaspoon onion powder
1/2 teaspoon garlic powder
1/2 teaspoon hot English mustard or
Dijon mustard
Salt and white pepper to taste
1 tablespoon fine breadcrumbs

Vegetables in Cheese Sauce
2lbs/1kg of fresh vegetables (cauliflower, cabbage, eggplant (aubergine, melongene), christophene (chocho), pumpkin, squash, broccoli, leeks, spinach.
2oz/60g butter
1/4 cup/4 tablespoons flour
2 cups 16floz/500ml milk
12oz/375g cheddar cheese
Pinch white pepper
Pinch onion powder

Pinch of garlic or garlic powder
1/2 teaspoon hot English mustard
powder or Dijon mustard
Salt and white pepper to taste
1 tablespoon fine breadcrumbs and some
grated cheese to garnish

1. Peel and half the christophenes lengthways. Scoop out the centre seed, making enough of a hollow to hold a reasonable amount of cheese sauce.
2. Boil in salted water until just tender. (6-8 mins) Put in a heatproof, buttered dish.
3. Melt butter in a small saucepan, add flour and cook for a couple of minutes over a medium heat, stirring.
4. Gradually add the milk, removing from the heat and beating each time it reaches boiling point, to blend.
5. Add dashes of white pepper, garlic powder, onion powder and mustard. Stir until nicely thickened and then add all the cheese. Cook on a medium heat for 3-5 minutes to melt cheese.
6. Fill each christophene to overflowing and top with breadcrumbs. Bake at 350F, 180C or Mark4 for 10-15 mins.

1. Clean, peel where necessary and cut the vegetables into large pieces. Boil in salted water for long enough that the vegetables are cooked but still a bit crunchy since they will continue to cook when they are baked for 10-15 minutes in the cheese sauce.
2. Cool and set aside in a shallow baking dish that has been greased with butter.
3. Melt butter in a small saucepan, blend in the flour and cook for a couple of minutes over a medium heat, stirring.
4. Gradually add the milk, removing from the heat and beating with a wooden spoon each time it reaches boiling point, to blend.
5. Add dashes of white pepper, garlic powder, onion powder and mustard. Stir until nicely thickened and add all the cheese. Cook on a medium heat for 3-5 minutes to melt cheese.

6. Pour over the cooked vegetables, sprinkle with the breadcrumbs and cheese and bake in a moderate oven 350F, 180C or Mark4 for 10-15 minutes or until lightly browned.

Serves 4-6

Roasted Eggplant & Tomatoes: Roasting tomatoes in the oven intensifies their wonderful flavour. They are delicious in sandwiches, or added to salads and pastas or to make pizza. This recipe, however, combines tomatoes with eggplants to produce a mouth-watering side dish.

Roasted Eggplant and Tomato Au Gratin: This is a very rich dish and can be served to compliment light main courses.

Roasted Vegetable Platter: A platter of mixed roasted vegetables is always popular. The tricky part, however, stems from the fact that some vegetables cook faster than others so, one must stagger the roasting.

Roasted Eggplant & Tomatoes

2lbs/1kg eggplant
1/2 cup 4floz/125ml olive oil
2 limes
2lbs/1kg tomatoes
Salt
Freshly ground pepper
Olive oil for brushing

1. Leave on the skin of the eggplant or peel as you prefer. Slice the eggplant and sprinkle generously with salt. Allow to drain in a collander for 5-10 minutes.
2. Rinse eggplant slices and marinate with some olive oil and a little lime juice.
3. Preheat a moderately cool oven 325F, 160C or Gas Mark 3
4. Wash and slice the tomatoes and place on an oiled baking sheet with salt and pepper to taste. Place the eggplant on the baking sheet.
5. Bake both the eggplant and tomato for 30-40 minutes or until nicely browned.

Oven Roasted Eggplant and Tomato Au Gratin

1/2lb/250g Eggplant
1/2lb/250g Tomatoes
1 tablespoon butter
2 tablespoons flour
2 cups 16floz/500ml milk
Dash of onion powder
Dash of white pepper
Dash of garlic powder
Pinch of hot mustard powder
1 cup 5oz/155g grated mozzarella cheese
Garnish: Parmesan cheese

1. Roast eggplant and tomatoes as in the preceeding recipe.
2. Melt butter in a small saucepan, add flour and cook for a couple of minutes over a medium heat, stirring.
3. Gradually add the milk, removing from the heat and beating each time it reaches boiling point, to blend.
4. Add dashes of white pepper, garlic powder, onion powder and mustard powder. Stir until nicely thickened and add all the cheese. Cook for 5 minutes.
5. In an 8" square, 2" deep oven proof dish layer the eggplant, tomato, eggplant and finish with the cheese sauce. Top with a little grated parmesan and bake in a moderate oven 325F, 160C or Gas Mark 3 for 15-20 minutes.

Roasted Vegetable Platter

1/2 cup 4floz/125ml olive oil
1 lime or 2 tablespoons balsamic vinegar
2 medium christophenes
8 small carrotts
1lb/500g pumpkin
2 medium ripe plantains
4 medium tomatoes
8 finger squash
1 large red onion
1 yellow sweet pepper
1 green sweet pepper
Salt and freshly ground pepper

1. Mix olive oil with lime juice or balsamic vinegar marinade.
2. Wash, peel and cut up the vegetables into bite sizes. Brush the plantain in olive oil. Place the christophene, carrots, pumpkin, tomatoes and squash in one zip lock bag and the sweet pepper, onion and mushrooms in another each with some marinade.
3. Heat oven at 325F, 160C or Gas Mark 3.
4. Place the christophene, carrots, pumpkin, squash and plantain on a baking sheet and bake for 35 minutes.
5. After 15 minutes, add the sweet pepper and onion on a baking sheet and bake for 20 minutes.
6. Serve all the vegetables on a large shallow, heated platter.

Serves 6-8

cole slaw

This recipe will give you an exotic and very tasty cole slaw. The fresh ginger option is delicious but only use a small thumbnail because the strong flavour can quite easily become overpowering.

1 1/4lbs/625g cabbage (white or mixed purple and white)
1/2lb/250g carrots
2/3 cup 5floz/150ml mayonnaise
2 teaspoons sugar (brown or light brown)
1/2-1 teaspoon salt
1/2 teaspoon yellow Caribbean hot pepper sauce or 1/2 teaspoon hot English mustard
1 medium finely chopped onion
1/4 cup/3 tablespoons raisins

1/2 cup 2oz/60g chopped nuts (almonds, pecans, peanuts or walnuts)
English mustard powder (optional)
1/4 cup 2floz/60ml water
A thumbnail of fresh ginger, grated (optional)

1. Cut off and remove the exposed leaves and the heart of the cabbage and discard. Finely slice the cabbage. Wash it thoroughly and soak in salted water for one hour. Drain well and chill to keep it crisp.
2. Peel and coarsely grate the carrots and add to the cabbage.
3. Mix the mayonnaise, sugar, pepper sauce and the water. Add the mayonnaise mixture, onions, raisins, nuts and ginger (if including this) to the cabbage and mix until thoroughly blended.
4. Keep in the fridge until ready to serve. Serves 8-10 people.

tomato salad/dressed cucumber/cucumber sandwiches

Tomato Salad: This salad makes tomatoes come alive. They spring their own juices and the left over juices can be bottled and used as a dressing at a later date.

Dressed Cucumber: Cucumber, lime and salt creates a wonderful "ménage a trois". This salad is delicious served as a side dish with fish or fish cakes.

Cucumber Sandwiches: The cucumber salad on this page is also the basis of very good cucumber sandwiches.

Tomato Salad
1lb/500g tomatoes
1 medium red onion thinly sliced
(optional)
Salt and freshly ground black pepper
1/2 cup/handful basil leaves thinly sliced
1/4 cup 4floz/125ml olive oil
2 tablespoons red wine or
balsamic vinegar
1 sprig fresh thyme, leaves picked off.

1. Wash and thickly slice tomatoes. Place on the serving dish along with the sliced onions if including.
2. Sprinkle with salt and pepper.
3. Sprinkle on the basil and thyme leaves.
4. Pour over the olive oil and vinegar.
5. Serve immediately or refrigerate for up to 2 hours.

Serves 4

Dressed Cucumber
1lb/500g cucumbers
1 teaspoon salt
1 tablespoon lime juice
1/2 tablespoon onion finely chopped
1/2 tablespoon white vinegar
1/2 teaspoon red hot pepper very finely chopped (optional).

1. Peel the cucumbers, leaving on some slivers of skin for colour and nutrition. Slice thinly.
2. Place in a bowl with salt, lime juice, onion, vinegar and hot pepper if using. Mix well and allow to stand for about 1/2 hour before serving.

Cucumber Sandwiches
Cucumber salad recipe on this page
1 loaf white sandwich bread
Mayonnaise
Butter

1. Slice crusts off bread and cover in a damp cloth to prevent the bread drying out.
2. Butter one side of the sandwich
3. Mayonnaise the other side.
4. Fill with cucumber salad.
5. Cut each sandwich in two or three pieces.
6. Garnish with parsley and serve. Makes 20-25 small sandwiches

seven layer salad

Unusual for a salad, this one is made the day before. It also travels well and this makes it an ideal salad to take along to "bring a dish" parties, picnics and boat trips. If you are taking it out, take along the tomatoes whole, since they need to be added just before serving. It should be kept cool.

4 cups (1 head) shredded iceburg lettuce
3-4 sticks celery, diced
6 hard boiled eggs, shelled and sliced
1-2 medium sweet peppers, chopped
4-6 medium carrots, grated
1/2 onion, thinly sliced
10 slices bacon, crispy fried
and crumbled
2 tablespoons sugar
2 cups 16floz/500ml mayonnaise
1/2 cup 4oz/125g grated cheddar cheese
1lb/500g tomatoes
Handful of fresh basil

1. When choosing the dish for this salad note that whereas it looks attractive in deep glass dish, as photographed opposite, a wider dish from which to help oneself to all layers, is easier.
2. Prepare the ingredients. Layer them in a salad bowl in the same order they are listed above.
3. Mix the sugar with the mayonnaise and spread on top, sealing the salad.
4. Sprinkle the cheese on top, cover with plastic wrap and refrigerate for at least 8 hours or up to 24.
5. Just before serving top with sliced tomato and fresh basil.

pasta salad

As with much of the world, pasta has become popular in the Caribbean. These two pasta salads are very quick and easy to make.

Cold Pasta Salad

8oz/250g rotini pasta
1-3 tablespoons finely chopped garlic
1/2 cup 4floz/125ml mayonnaise
Salt and freshly ground pepper to taste
1 1/2lbs/500g fresh tomatoes, diced
2 cups 1oz/30g chopped fresh basil
2 green topped spring onions

1. Bring a large pan of salted water to boil and add the pasta. Boil until the pasta is tender but not soft.
2. Drain, cool slightly and toss with the garlic, mayonnaise, salt and freshly ground black pepper.
3. When well mixed add the diced tomato, chopped spring onions and fresh basil, mixing as little as possible to blend so that the tomato and basil don't get coated in too much mayonnaise and lose their colour.
4. Chill and serve garnished with fresh basil. Does not keep well overnight.

Serves 6-8 as a side dish

Warm Pasta Salad

1 1/2lbs/500g fresh tomatoes, diced
Salt and pepper to taste
1/2-1 tablespoon finely chopped garlic
1 cup 1oz/30g chopped fresh basil
4 tablespoons olive oil
1 tablespoon balsamic vinegar
8oz/250g rotini pasta
1/2 cup 2oz/60g parmesan cheese
Garnish: Fresh basil

1. Chop up the fresh tomatoes, sprinkle with salt, garlic, basil, olive oil, vinegar and freshly ground black pepper. Mix well, squeezing with clean hands if you like.
2. Meanwhile, bring a large pan of salted water to boil and add the pasta. Boil until the pasta is tender but not soft.
3. Drain pasta, return to the pan, and add the tomato mixture. Return the pan to the heat. Toss until the tomato and pasta are well blended and the mixture is hot.
4. Serve hot with grated parmesan cheese garnished with sprigs of fresh basil.

Serves 4 as a main course

potato salad

This is a very attractive potato salad. Although photographed opposite in a flat dish, if it is not mixed up, it also looks superb in a deep glass dish with an increased number of layers.

2 lbs English potatoes
4 eggs
1 cup 8floz/250ml mayonnaise
1 teaspoon hot English mustard powder
or 1/2 teaspoon yellow pepper sauce
2 tablespoons onion, grated
Salt and pepper to taste
1/2 cup 4floz/125ml water
1/2 cup/ bunch parsley finely chopped
1/2 cup/4-6 scallions finely chopped
2 tablespoons/2 large sprigs fresh thyme
leaves

2 tablespoons/2 large sprigs fresh
marjoram, finely chopped

1. Peel and boil the potatoes until just
   tender in salted water. Drain and cool.
2. Boil the eggs for 10 minutes, cool and
   shell.
3. Mix the mayonnaise, mustard or pepper
   sauce, salt, pepper, onion and water in a
   small pouring jug.
4. Prepare the herbs.
5. Slice the eggs and potatoes.
6. Place a layer of about a third of the
   sliced potatoes in the serving dish,
   followed by a layer of sliced eggs, pour
   over a 1/3 of the mayonnaise sauce and
   sprinkle with a 1/3 of the chopped
   herbs. Repeat twice.
7. The salad may be left in distinct layers
   or mixed up, whichever is your
   preference.
8. Cover and refrigerate for a couple of
   hours before serving.

Serves 6-8

hoppin' john/black beans and rice

The "meaty" and nutritious black beans are best known for their role in Cuban cuisine. They are either prepared into a hearty stew and served with fluffy white rice or cooked with the rice. This attractive black and white combination is known colloquially as Moores and Christians.

The cooking time of dried beans is reduced if they are soaked overnight in water with a pinch of soda bicarbonate (baking soda).

Hoppin' John
1 cup black eye peas
10 cups water
1 lb/500g 4-6 medium tomatoes
1 1/2 cups 12floz/357ml rice
1 medium onions finely chopped
1/4lb/125g salt meat
Sprigs of thyme and margaram
1 fresh hot chilli or bonnet pepper
1 tablespoon butter
Salt and freshly ground pepper to taste

1. Cook the dried peas in 6 cups water very rapidly for about 10-15 minutes. Reduce to simmer for about 40 mins or until tender. Drain the peas and rinse in cold water.
2. Pour boiling water over the tomatoes. Peel and dice them. Wash the rice well in a bowl of water and drain.
3. Heat the butter and sauté the onions until beginning to brown. Add the tomatoes, washed rice, cooked black eye peas, herbs, whole fresh pepper, salt beef, four cups of water, salt meat, a little salt to taste and freshly ground pepper.
4. Bring to the boil, cover and cook on medium heat for 5 minutes.
5. Reduce heat to low and simmer until the water is steamed out (20-25mins).

Serves 4

Black Beans & Rice
1 cup 8oz/250g dried black beans
10 cups 80floz/2.5l water
1 1/2 cups 12floz/375ml rice
2 tablespoons olive oil
1 medium onions finely chopped
Small piece salt pork finely chopped
1 teaspoon garlic finely chopped
1/2 cup 1 sweet pepper finely chopped
1/2 cup 2 tomatoes peeled and chopped
Salt and pepper to taste

1. Put the beans in the colander and pour boiling water over them until the water runs clear. Transfer to a large saucepan along with 6 cups water. Bring to the boil and then reduce the heat to low. Skim off any scum, cover and simmer until the beans are tender but still intact. (1-2 hours). Drain the beans and rinse in cold water.
2. Wash the rice well and drain.
3. In a heavy saucepan, heat the olive oil and sauté the onion and salt pork. When the onion has softened, add the garlic and sweet pepper, sautéing for a couple of minutes, and then add the rice, tomatoes, salt, pepper, and 4 cups of water.
4. Bring to the boil, cover and reduce the heat to medium low until the water is completely absorbed.

Serves 4-6

steamed rice/pigeon peas & rice

Perfect Steamed Rice: Not all plain steamed rice is created equal - subtle seasoning and thorough washing makes the world of difference.
Pigeon Peas & Rice: Peas and rice is a dish that is eaten throughout the Caribbean. Pigeon peas are related to the tender green sweet peas but are much higher in protein and vitamins, making this a very nutritious dish.

Perfect Steamed Rice
4 cups 32floz/960ml water
3/4 teaspoon salt
1/2 chicken stock cube
1 tablespoon butter
1 small onion finely chopped
1 1/2 cups 12floz/360ml rice

Pigeon Peas & Rice
2 cups 11oz/345g fresh/frozen pigeon
peas
6 cups 48floz/1.45l water
Bouquet garni of fresh thyme, marjoram
and chives
1/4lb/125g salt beef or salt pork
1 tablespoon butter
2 cups 8floz/250ml rice
1 large tomato, blanched, peeled and
chopped up
1 tablespoon lime juice
Red pepper sauce to taste

1. Put the water, salt, stock cube, butter and onion in a medium saucepan and bring to the boil.
2. Wash the rice thoroughly in a bowl of water, strain and repeat.
3. Add to the pan, whether it's boiling yet or not.
4. Boil uncovered on medium heat for 10 minutes.
5. Cover tightly and reduce heat to low. Let it steam until all the water is absorbed (15-20 minutes).

Using Fresh Pigeon Peas
1. Cover and boil the peas, herbs and salt beef in four cups of water for about 1/2 hour. If you are not using salt meat, add salt to taste.
2. Wash the rice and drain. Add the rice, 2 more cups of water, butter, tomato and lime juice.
3. Bring to the boil, cover and cook on medium heat for 5 minutes.
4. Reduce heat to low and let it simmer until all the water is steamed out (20-25 minutes).

Using Dried Pigeon Peas
1. If using dried pigeon peas, use 1 cup to peas and increase the water to 7 cups and cook the dried peas very rapidly for about 10-15 minutes and then reduce to simmer for about 40 mins or until tender.
2. Proceed with the recipe as above.

breadfruit

Captain William Bligh was chosen to lead an expedition to the South Seas to bring the breadfruit to the Caribbean. On his first attempt, his devotion to the breadfruit saplings and neglect of his crew's water needs lead to the famous mutiny on the Bounty. Cast overboard, Captain Bligh made his way hundreds of miles to safety in an open boat. On his second attempt in 1793 he sailed into Jamaica's Port Royal Harbour with a ship so crowded with beautiful leafy breadfruit saplings that the Jamaicans rowed out toward "the ship that have bush". Today large, lush breadfruit trees grow throughout the Caribbean bearing the football like starchy staple that has kept hunger away from many a door.

Breadfruit in Butter Sauce
1/2 medium breadfruit
1/2 small onion
1 tablespoon olive oil
4 oz/125g butter
1-2 medium onions, cut in rings
1 tablespoon garlic finely chopped
1 medium 16floz/500ml tin whole tomatoes, drained and sliced
1/4 cup/3 tablespoons parsley, diced
1 tablespoon lime juice
Salt and pepper to taste
1 cup 8oz/250ml water
Red pepper sauce to taste.
Garnish: fresh parsley, chopped

1. Cut the breadfruit, remove the seeds in the core and peel. Boil in salted water with a little onion and oil, over a high heat until tender and drain.
2. Meanwhile, melt the butter in a frying pan and lightly brown the onion rings. Add the garlic, tomatoes, parsley, lime juice, salt and pepper. Continue to sauté for a couple of minutes. Add the water, bring to the boil and simmer for 5-10 minutes.
3. Slice the cooled breadfruit and place in a serving dish. Pour the butter sauce over the breadfruit.
4. Garnish with chopped fresh parsley.

Serves 4

Pickled Breadfruit
1/2 medium breadfruit
1 tablespoon oil
Souse pickle:
1 lb/500g small cucumber, peeled, deseeded and very finely chopped
1/4 cup 1 small onion finely chopped
Salt to taste
1/3 cup parsley finely chopped
Fresh hot pepper very finely chopped to taste (about 1/4 deseeded pepper)
1 medium sweet pepper finely chopped
3-6 tablespoons lime juice, to taste
Garnish: fresh parsley, sweet pepper

1. Cut the breadfruit, remove the seeds in the core and peel. Boil in salted water and oil, over a high heat until just tender. Drain and cool.
2. Meanwhile prepare the pickle ingredients and mix well. Remove any seeds from the cucumber. Put enough salt and lime juice to make a nice acid salty pickly since the bland breadfruit quickly counteracts it.
3. Slice the breadfruit, mix into the pickle. Place in a serving dish and garnish with parsley and sweet pepper rings.

Serves 4-6

Breadfruit Chips
Breadfruit
Canola oil for frying
Seasoned salt

1. Quarter, core and peel the breadfruit.
2. Slice as thinly as possible. Fry in deep oil until brown and crispy.
3. Sprinkle with seasoned salt and serve.

orange sweet potato bake

Arrowroot flour, an alternative for cornstarch is a very pure form of starch without smell, taste or allergenic properties. It is grown and produced in small quantities on the island of St. Vincent, where the plant is indigenous. Used as a thickener of gravies and sauces, in baby foods and as a cure for stomach ailments, it was a major export of St. Vincent in the first half of the twentieth century. Having declined dramatically, in 2002 a strategic plan for the revitalization of the arrowroot industry has been put in place.

3-4lbs/1.5-2kg sweet potatoes
Salt
2 tablespoons oil
1 tablespoon grated orange rind
1 cup 8floz/250ml orange juice
2 tablespoons lime juice
2 tablespoons cornstarch or arrowroot
2oz/60g butter
2 tablespoons brown sugar
2 tablespoons minced preserved ginger

1 tablespoon preserved ginger syrup
(Fresh ginger boiled with 1/4 cup sugar
and a little water for 1/2 hour will also
work)
1 cup 4oz/125g sliced or chopped raw
almonds.

A note about sweet potatoes
Caribbean sweet potatoes have a white or very pale yellow starchy texture, as shown on the far left on page 81. Sometimes called yams outside of the Caribbean, they are very different from the yellow or orange, waxy textured sweet potato commonly sold in North America.

1. Boil sweet potatoes in their skins well covered in water with oil and salt, until tender. About 20 minutes. Drain and cool.
2. In a saucepan, boil the orange rind, orange juice, lime juice, corn starch, butter, sugar, minced ginger and ginger syrup until thick.
3. Peel and slice the potatoes and arrange in overlapping slices on a 12" shallow dish.
4. Pour the sauce over the potato slices and top with the almonds.
5. Bake at 350F, 180C or Gas Mark 4 for about 20 minutes until the sauce is bubbling and the nuts are toasted.

Serves 10-12

yam in butter sauce

Yams were discovered in the Caribbean when Colombus arrived here. This root crop comes in various sizes and many strange shapes, with a rough dark brown skin and white or creamy coloured starchy flesh. Not to be confused with the starchy Caribbean sweet potatoes which are sometimes referred to as yams in North America. The delicate and slightly nutty flavour of yam is perfectly suited to this very simple recipe. There is no need for garlic, herbs and lime juice like the Creole butter sauce served over breadfruit. This dish goes especially well with fried fish.

3lbs/750g yam
3oz/90g butter
2 small onions, cut in rings
1 tin 16floz/500ml whole tomatoes
A few dashes worcestershire sauce
Salt and pepper to taste
1/2 cup 4floz/125ml water
Pepper sauce to taste

1. Peel and cut up the yam, under running water, dropping each piece into a saucepan of salted water immediately. Be sure to keep the peeled yamcovered in water at all times to prevent it discolouring. Wash hands and lower arms thoroughly as an organic chemical in yams skin can cause itching. You can wear gloves or rub your hands in oil to prevent any chance of this. Boil until just tender. Be careful not to overcook.
2. Meanwhile, melt the butter in a small frying pan and lightly brown the onion rings.
3. Drain and slice the tomatoes and add to the onions. Continue to sauté for a couple of minutes, seasoning to taste with salt and pepper.
4. Add the water and bring to the boil and simmer for a couple of minutes.
5. Slice the yam and arrange in a serving dish. Pour over the butter sauce.
6. Serve hot.

Serves 6.

macaroni cheese

One of the nations that has influenced the Caribbean cuisine is of course the closest, the USA. Referred to in many islands simply as "pie", macaroni cheese is standard fare and always a winner, especially with children. There are several variations to this dish. It can also be made with different kinds of pasta such as penne or rotini. Adding 2 small tins of tuna is also an option, to make a one pot meat served with salad.

8oz/250g macaroni
1 tablespoon butter or margarine
1 1/2 lbs/675g sharp chedder cheese, grated
1 egg
1 cup 8floz/240ml evaporated milk
1 small grated onion
1 teaspoon hot English mustard
1 tablespoon yellow mustard
1 teaspoon white pepper
1 teaspoon salt

1/2 teaspoon red pepper sauce or cayenne pepper (optional)
1 1/2 tablespoons tomato ketchup
1 finely chopped sweet pepper (optional)
Garnish:
2 tablespoons fine breadcrumbs
2 teaspoons butter
2 tablespoons grated chedder cheese

1. Bring water to the boil and add the broken up macaroni or macaroni elbows and salt. Boil it uncovered until it is just tender but not overcooked (about 8 minutes).
2. Preheat a moderately hot oven 350F, 180C or Gas Mark 4.
3. Drain the macaroni thoroughly, put it back into the same hot saucepan it was cooked in and mix in the butter.
4. Grate the cheese and mix it in with the macaroni a bit at a time, while it is still warm.
5. Whisk the egg until fluffy and add the milk, onion powder, white pepper, salt, pepper sauce and mustard. Pour in with the macaroni and mix.
6. Place in a greased oven proof casserole dish. Top with a little butter, some grated cheese and fine breadcrumbs. Bake in the centre of the oven for about 30-45 minutes depending on the depth of the dish.

ground provision pies

Ground provisions play an important role in the diet of West Indians. Often cited by centenarians as a reason for their longevity. Sweet potatoes and yams in particular are good sources of energy - they are slowly metabolised by the body and contain many vitamins and minerals. One of the advantages of ground provision pies is that they can be made ahead of time and travel well when one is contributing to a get-together.

Sweet Potato Pie

2 1/2 lbs/1.25kg sweet potatoes
1 teaspoon salt
1 tablespoon oil
1 egg
4oz/125g butter
1 cup 8floz/250ml milk
Salt and pepper to taste
Garnish: Fine breadcrumbs, grated cheese and a tablespoon of butter

1. Peel and cut up the sweet potatoes and put them into water immediately to avoid discolouring. Make sure that the saucepan has enough water to cover them, add the oil and a teaspoon of salt and bring to the boil. Simmer on a medium heat until soft, (about 20 minutes).
2. Whisk the egg. Drain the sweet potatoes and while they are still hot add the egg, butter, milk and salt and pepper to taste. Mash using a hand blender or potato masher.
3. Grease a casserole dish and fill with the mashed potato mixture.
4. Sprinkle the top of the potato with some fine breadcrumbs and a few dabs of butter. Bake in a moderate oven for 25 minutes.

Serves 4-6

Yam Pie

3lbs/1.5kg yam
2 tablespoons butter
3/4 to 1 1/2 cups 6-12floz/190-350ml milk (depending on moistness of yam)
Salt and white pepper
Onion powder
Garlic powder
1 egg
8oz/250g grated chedder cheese (optional)

1. Peel and thickly slice the yam, under running water. Place in a saucepan of salted water immediately to prevent discolouring. Wash hands and over arms thoroughly as some yam skin causes itching. Boil until soft, (about 15 mins).
2. While still hot, drain and mash the yam. Then melt the butter with the smaller quantity of milk, salt, white pepper, onion powder and garlic powder in a small saucepan. Whisk the egg and add to the war mmilk mixture.
3. Then mix well with the mashed yam and grated cheese, ensuring there are no lumps. The texture should be more moist than mashed potatoes as yam dries out when it is baked. Add milk if needed. Let it stand and mash again.
4. Place in a baking dish and top with a little butter and some fine breadcrumbs. Bake 350F, 180C or Gas 4 for 1/2 hour.

Serves 4-6

Easy Corn Pie

2 eggs
2 tablespoons milk
1-2 tablespoons brown sugar
1/2 teaspoon vanilla essence
1 can 15oz/425g cream style corn
1 can 15oz/425g whole kernel corn drained
2 tablespoons butter (softened)
Dash of Angostura bitters (optional)

1. Beat eggs and add the ingredients in the order of listing. Mix lightly. If you want a light "souffle" type of corn pie, separate the eggs, beat the eggs whites until stiff and fold into the rest of the ingredients including the egg yolks.
2. Pour into buttered casserole dish. Bake at 180C, 350F Gas mark 3 until firm. (about 15 minutes.)

Serves 6-8

balls

Yam and sweet potato balls are a little more trouble but much more impressive yam and sweet potato pie. They can be made the day before and baked or fried just before serving, which is convenient. These balls are most enjoyable when served with a main dish that has plenty of gravy or sauce. Little chunks of cheese can be pushed into the center of the balls before rolling in the egg and breadcrumbs. A ricer is great for mashing sweet potato and breadfruit. It takes out the lumps and lightens the mixture.

Sweet Potato Balls
1 1/2lb/750g sweet potato
1 teaspoon salt
1 tablespoon oil
1oz/30g butter
2 eggs
Freshly ground black pepper
1 cup 4oz/125g very fine breadcrumbs
Olive oil for brushing or frying
12-16 small cubes of cheese (optional)

1. Peel and cut up the sweet potatoes. Boil in a large covered saucepan with plenty of water, salt and 1 tablespoon of oil until tender (15-20 mins).
2. Drain well and while hot mash with the butter and freshly ground pepper.
3. Whisk one egg and mix into the potato.
4. Whisk another egg and set aside. Blend the breadcrumbs and flour in a small pan.
5. Using a teaspoon to scoop out the mixture, roll into approx 12 balls. You may push a chunk of cheese into the centre. Dip each ball in the egg and roll in the breadcrumb and flour mixture.
6. Refrigerate until ready to use.
7. When ready to bake, brush with oil and bake in at 200C, 400F or Gas Mark 5 for 20-25 minutes or shallow fry in oil until golden brown.
8. Garnish with sprigs of fresh herbs and serve hot.

Serves 6-8

Yam Balls
2lbs/1kg yam
2 eggs
1/2 cup 4oz/125g grated cheese
2oz/60g butter
White pepper and salt to taste
2 teaspoons garlic powder
1 tablespoon onion powder
1 cup 2oz/60g very fine breadcrumbs
12-16 small cubes of cheese (optional)

1. Peel, cut up and boil the yam in plenty of salted water until cooked. To avoid the itching that yams may cause wash your hands and lower arms thoroughly after peeling or wear gloves.
2. While it is still hot, mash the yam with the cheese, butter, white pepper, salt, onion powder and garlic powder.
3. Whisk one egg and add to the yam.
4. Whisk another egg and set aside. Place the breadcrumbs in a shallow pan.
5. Flour your hands and roll the yam into balls. You may push a chunk of cheese into the centre. Dip each ball in the beaten egg and roll in the breadcrumbs.
6. Refrigerate until ready to use.
7. Brush with oil and bake at 375F, 180C or Gas Mark 3 for about 20 minutes or shallow fry in oil.
8. Garnish with sprigs of fresh herbs and serve hot.

Serves 6-8

Breadfruit Balls
1/2 medium breadfruit
2 eggs
1oz/30g butter
Salt and black pepper
1 tablespoon onion powder
1 teaspoon garlic powder
Oil for brushing or frying
1 cup 2oz/60g very fine breadcrumbs
12-16 small cubes of cheese (optional)

1. Boil the breadfruit until it is cooked but still firm. If it is too soft it will not hold well in the balls.
2. While it is still hot, mash the breadfruit with butter, onion powder, garlic powder, black pepper and salt.
3. Whisk one egg until light and fluffy and mix in to the mashed breadfruit.
4. Whisk another egg and set aside and place the breadcrumbs in a shallow pan.
5. Flour your hands and roll the breadfruit into balls. You may push a chunk of cheese into the centre. Dip each ball in the beaten egg and roll in the breadcrumbs. Place in a buttered oven proof dish and refrigerate until ready to use.
6. Brush with olive oil and bake at 375F, 180C or Gas Mark 4 for about 20 minutes or shallow fry in oil until golden brown.
7. Garnish with sprigs of fresh herbs and serve hot.

Serves 6-8

curried fig/pickled fig

Referred to in many islands as 'fig', and not to be confused with smaller members of the banana family, green bananas are another healthy starch alternative enjoyed by West Indians. The bunches of thin, hard and bright green bananas are sold in markets and supermarkets, year round. With carbohydrates that are slowly metabolized by the body, they are also full of vitamins and minerals, most notably iron. When boiled without peeling they give off a sticky black sap that is difficult to wash off the saucepan, so it is best to peel them first.

Curried Fig

16-20 green bananas
Curry Sauce:
1 tablespoon olive oil
1 onion finely chopped
1 tablespoon garlic finely chopped
1/2 cup/7 tablespoons curry powder
2-3 cups 16-24floz/500-700ml stock
5 cardamom pods, whole
2 cups 16floz/500ml unsweetened
coconut milk (Coconut milk powder
mixed with boiling water works well)
2 bay leaves
1 teaspoon ground cumin
1 teaspoon ground ginger
Salt to taste

1. Oil hands before peeling green bananas to avoid getting hands stained with sap. The sap from green bananas stains clothes and is very hard to remove. Peel the green bananas. Cut a slit down the length of the banana skin, cut off either end of the banana and attempt to split the skin open and pull it off. If this fails, simply peel the banana with a knife. Boil in salted water immediatley, to avoid discolouration, until tender.
2. In a medium to large saucepan, heat the oil and sauté the onions and curry powder for a couple of minutes. Add the garlic and sauté for a short while longer.
3. Pour in 2 cups of the reserved stock, cardamom pods, coconut milk, bay leaves and cumin. Simmer on a medium heat for about 10 minutes.
4. Once the curry sauce is a nice creamy consistency, taste and add salt and more stock if necessary. Add the green bananas and simmer for a further 10-15 minutes. Be careful to stir as little as possible so the bananas remain in nice pieces.
5. Remove the 5 cardamom pods if possible and serve.

Pickled Fig

16-20 green bananas
Souse Pickle:
1 lb/500g small cucumbers, peeled and
very finely chopped
1/4 cup/1 medium onion, finely chopped
salt to taste
1/2 cup/5 tablespoons parsley, finely
chopped
Fresh hot pepper, very finely chopped, to
taste
1 medium sweet pepper, finely chopped
3-6 tablespoons lime juice, to taste
Garnish: Parsley and sweet pepper
rings

1. Boil bananas as in curried fig recipe.
2. Meanwhile, prepare the pickle ingredients and mix well. Remove any seeds from the cucumber. Put enough salt and lime juice to give the pickle a good twang, since the green bananas soak it up quickly.
3. Place bananas in pickle in a bowl and refrigerate. Should be served within 2 or 3 hours.
4. Place in a serving dish and garnish with parsley and sweet pepper rings.

snapperpepperthyme

main courses

barbecued or seared fish/fresh tuna salad

Barbecued or Seared Fish: One of the secrets to the successful preparation of seared or barbecued fish is to use an oil-based marinade. Remember, too, that fish needs very little time over the heat in order to be cooked through. One final tip to delicious barbecued fish: it is much tastier when placed directly over the heat in a folding fish rack, wrapping in foil tends to steam the fish.

Fresh Tuna Salad: It is a good idea to do all the preparation ahead of time and simply put the salad together just before serving. You can also put out all the ingredients in bowls and let everyone make their own salad.

Barbecued or Seared Fish
6 servings of fish fillets (3-4lbs/1.5-2kg) suggested varieties include tuna, dorado/mahi mahi, salmon, barracuda, snapper, wahoo, or marlin
2 tablespoons of Caribbean seasoning or basil pesto
2 cloves fresh garlic finely chopped
1/2 cup 4floz/125ml olive oil
1 lime
1 teaspoon salt
1 cup 8floz/250ml water

1. Marinate the fillets of fish in the lime, salt and water for about 10 minutes.
2. Rinse and drain fish.
3. Mix seasoning or pesto, garlic and oil in a shallow dish and place fish in marinade, coating well. Marinate at room temperature for at least 1/2 hour or overnight in the fridge.
4. If possible, remove from the fridge a couple of hours before cooking.
5. Place the fish in a folding fish rack. Barbecue over a high heat for 2-4 minutes on each side, depending on the type of fish and how rare you prefer it. If you are searing it, heat a pan without any oil, put in the marinated fish, turn after a minute or two and sear the other side. Serve immediately.

Serves 6

Fresh Tuna Salad
6 servings barbecued or seared tuna
6 small to medium potatoes
3/4 cup 6floz/190ml olive oil
2 tablespoons lime juice
6 medium tomatoes
2 tablespoons red wine or balsamic vinegar
Freshly ground black pepper
Salt
2 medium thinly sliced red onions
1 cup 1oz/30g fresh basil

1. Follow recipe for barbecued or seared tuna up to just before cooking it. (#4)
2. Boil the potatoes in their skins until just cooked. Peel, slice and sauté until golden brown in 1/4 cup olive oil. Sprinkle with salt and set aside.
3. Wash and quarter tomatoes and place in a bowl with 1/4 cup olive oil, 2 tablespoons vinegar, salt, freshly ground black pepper, thinly sliced red onion and 1/4 cup thinly sliced fresh basil. Toss and set aside.
4. Wash and dry the lettuce. Thinly slice half of the basil and mix with the lettuce.
5. Combine 1/4 cup olive oil, 1 tablespoon lime juice, salt and pepper and set aside.
6. Just before serving cook the tuna, preferably rare, as explained in the preceeding recipe for seared or barbecued fish (#5).

6 main course portions (about a lb/500g) lettuce (Use any lettuce except iceburg, and include lettuce varieties that tend to be spicy, such as rocket/arugula)
6 hard boiled eggs, peeled and sliced
1 cup (approx 24) pitted black olives, in halves. Whenever possible, use the dried, cured black olives as they are extremely flavourful.

7. Put the lime dressing on the lettuce and basil mixture and place lettuce in the centre of each plate.
8. Arrange the tomato and onion mixture, sauté potatoes, olives and egg slices around the outside of each plate. Place the cooked tuna on the top of the lettuce, garnish with remaining fresh basil and serve immediately. Serve the residual dressing from the tomatoes in a sauceboat.

Serves 6

fish in white sauce

This dish can be made ahead of time, stored in the fridge and baked just before serving. It is especially delicious when served with boiled or mashed potatoes and vegetables, such as carrots, pumpkin, or string beans with almonds. It may be enhanced by including seafood such as shrimp and lobster.

4 servings of fish fillets such as dorado, wahoo, salmon or any firm fish
2 cups 16floz/500ml water
1 teaspoon dried mixed herbs or a tablespoon fresh thyme, parsley and marjoram finely chopped
1 tablespoon onion powder or grated onion
1 teaspoon garlic powder or one clove garlic finely chopped
1/2 stock cube, chicken or fish

1/2 teaspoon of salt
White pepper to taste
2 tablespoons margarine or butter
1/4 cup/4 tablespoons flour
2 cups 16floz/500ml milk
1 tablespoon parmesan cheese
1/4 cup/4 tablespoons dry white wine (optional)
3 hard-boiled eggs, shelled (optional)
Garnish: Fine breadcrumbs and parmesan cheese

1. Place the fish fillets in a saucepan with water, garlic, onion powder, salt, white pepper, herbs and the 1/2 stock cube. Bring to the boil and simmer for 3-5 minutes or until cooked (Fish needs very little cooking and if overcooked can be tough).
2. Remove the fish from the stock and set aside. Reserve the stock in a jug.
3. Over a medium to high heat melt the butter or margarine and add the flour to make a fairly dry roux. Gradually add the milk. Remove from the heat each time the milk comes to the boil, beating with a wooden spoon, to blend. Add 2 cups of the fish stock, the herbs, the wine and parmesan cheese. Simmer over a medium to high heat, stirring until the sauce thickens.

4. Option 1
   Remove from the heat, break the fish into chunks and add to the sauce. Preheat a moderate oven 350F, 180C or Gas Mark 4. Grease a casserole dish, slice and arrange the hard boiled eggs in the bottom and pour the fish mixture over. Top with a little butter and some fine breadcrumbs or parmesan cheese. Bake for 20 minutes.
4. Option 2
   Pipe four portions of hot mashed potatoes. Heat the 4 servings of poached fish and place on top of the mashed potatoes. Pour over the sauce. Place the vegetables on the plate and serve immediately.

Serves 4

blackened fish

It doesn't get much easier than blackened fish A delicious, spicy coating on moist tender fish. One of the important secrets to its success is to be careful not to overcook the fish. Blackened fish powder is a supermarket product, but this recipe gives ingredients that are more easily available and found in most kitchen cupboards. If you do use packaged blackened fish seasoning, you probably need to add an equal amount of flour as it is generally too strong. White steamed rice and salad go well with this.

4 serving sized fish fillets or enough
smaller fillets to serve 4 people
1 lime
Salt
2 cups 16floz/500ml water
1/4 cup/3-4 tablespoons chilli powder
1 tablespoon freshly ground black
pepper
1 tablespoon paprika
1/4 cup/3-4 tablespoons flour
Small amount of oil for searing

Lime Butter
2 oz/60g butter
2 tablespoons lime juice
Salt and pepper to taste

1. Place fish fillets in a bowl along with the water, juice of one lime and salt. Allow to soak for 20-30 minutes.
2. In a shallow dish or pan, mix the chilli powder, freshly ground black pepper, paprika and flour. Drain the fish and shake off excess moisture. Roll each fillet in the spiced flour, shaking off any excess. This can be done the day before cooking and refrigerated. Leaving it to "dry marinate" probably improves the spicy flavours in the fish.
3. Heat a thin layer of oil in a large frying pan on a high heat and sear the fish for 1-2 minutes on each side depending on the thickness of the fish fillet.
4. Serve with lime butter.

1. Melt the butter in a small saucepan. Add the lime juice and season with salt and pepper.
2. Pour into a flat dish and chill to set.
3. Cut into little wedges when ready to serve.

kedgeree

Originally an English breakfast dish made with smoked fish, this recipe uses fresh fish and is an easy and nutritious one pot meal for anytime of day. Although this uses raw rice it can be easily converted to use up leftover rice by sprinkling in the powdered turmeric and curry powder when frying up the rice. Serve with tomato and cucumber salads (page 56)

2 cups 16floz/500ml rice
1 tablespoon chilli or olive oil
2 tablespoons curry powder
1 tablespoon turmeric powder
4 cups 32floz/1l water
1 chicken stock cube
Pinch of salt
2lbs/1kg of fresh fish fillets
1 lime
1 teaspoon salt
1 tablespoon olive oil

1 medium onions finely chopped
4 hard boiled eggs
1/2 cup/small bunch parsley
Garnish: 1/2 cup, small bunch parsley finely chopped

1. Place the rice in a large bowl of water, wash thoroughly and drain.
2. Place the oil in a large saucepan and sauté the curry powder and turmeric for a couple of minutes. Add the washed raw rice and fry for a few minutes, stirring periodically. Add the chicken stock cube (crumbled), water and salt. Bring to the boil, cover and reduce the heat to low. Cook until all the liquid is completely absorbed (15-20 minutes). Turn out on the serving platter to cool and prevent further cooking.
3. Meanwhile, cut up the fish into bite size pieces, soak in a bowl of 2 cups of water, the juice of one lime and a teaspoon of salt for about 20 minutes, drain, rinse and pat dry.
4. Heat the olive oil in a large shallow frying pan and sauté the onion until soft. Add the rice and sauté for 10 minutes mixing well with onion.
5. Shell and slice the eggs.
6. Add the fish chunks, chopped parsley and sliced eggs and cook for about 10 minutes. Turn the mixture carefully so as not to break up the fish and eggs too much and yet blend them well with the rice.
7. Serve garnished with chopped parsley.

stewed down salt fish & cou cou

Stewed down salt fish can also be served with rice, breadfruit or yam. This cou cou recipe is different in that the corn meal is blended with cold water ahead of cooking it with the okras. This makes it smooth and much quicker to prepare.

Stewed Down Salt Fish
1lb boneless salted cod
2oz/60g butter
2 medium onions, thinly sliced
2 tablespoons finely chopped garlic
1 sweet pepper thinly sliced
2 cups 16oz/500ml tinned tomatoes or
2lbs/1kg peeled fresh tomatoes, sliced
1 tablespoon curry powder
1 sprig fresh thyme
1 sprig fresh marjoram
2 sprigs fresh parsley, finely chopped
1/2 cups 20floz/600ml water
Salt and freshly ground pepper to taste
1 teaspoon pepper sauce
4 hard-boiled eggs (optional)

Cou Cou
2 1/2 cups 12oz corn meal
1-2 teaspoons salt
Water
8oz/250g okras
2 tablespoons chopped onion
2oz/60g butter

1. Boil salt fish in plenty of water for 20 minutes. If still too salty, repeat. Drain salt fish, break into wedges, check for bones and set aside.
2. Heat butter and sauté the onion. When beginning to brown, add garlic, salt fish and sweet pepper and sauté for a further 3 minutes.
3. Add tomatoes, curry powder, herbs, water, pepper sauce and black pepper and simmer uncovered for 15 minutes to an hour or until tender. Salt to taste.
4. If adding eggs, shell and slice them and add to the salt fish about 10 minutes before its finished cooking.

1. Process the corn meal and 1 teaspoon salt with 3 cups of water in a blender.
2. Cut the tops off the okras, wash and slice thinly into circles. Place okras in a medium saucepan with 3 cups of water, and chopped onion. Bring to the boil and simmer for 10 minutes. Strain into a heat proof jug and place the okras back into the saucepan along with the butter and blended corn meal.
3. Place the saucepan with the corn meal over a medium heat and very gradually add the okra water, stirring to blend.
4. Once all okra water is added, lower the heat, cover and steam.

Serves 4

Serves 4

chilli shrimp

This delicious dish is best made with raw shrimp, as they tend to absorb the flavour of the sauce better than pre-cooked shrimp. Be careful, however, not to overcook them as they may become quite rubbery. If one does use pre-cooked shrimp, simply add them when the sauce is ready, and cook just long enough for them to be heated through. This recipe, which is delicious served with steamed white rice or pasta preceeded by a salad appetizer, can also be made with fish.

4 servings raw medium/large shrimp
(2lbs/1kg with the shell on or 1.5lbs/750g shelled)
2/3cup milk
1/4 cup/3 tablespoons olive oil
1 medium finely chopped onions
1 tablespoon chopped garlic
1 large or 2 small finely chopped sweet peppers
1 large can 32floz/960ml of tomatoes
2 tablespoons chilli powder
1 teaspoon ground cumin

1 teaspoon salt
1 teaspoon sugar
1 tablespoon fresh lime juice
Garnish: Fresh coriander (chardonbeni)

1. Shell, de-vein and wash the raw shrimp. Soak in fresh milk and place in the fridge. For cooked shrimp omit this step.
2. Heat the olive oil in a medium saucepan and sauté the onion until it begins to brown. Add the garlic and sweet pepper and sauté for two minutes. Add the finely chopped tomatoes along with the liquid they come in. (A hand blender is great for chopping up tomatoes for sauces, take a couple of tomatoes out to make room and chop with a hand blender in the can. Hand chop the couple you took out.) Add the chilli powder, cumin, lime juice, salt and sugar.
3. Cover tightly and simmer on a medium low heat for about 1/2 hour.
4. Rinse and drain the shrimp and add them to the sauce. Cover and continue to simmer for 5 to 10 minutes depending on the size of your shrimp.

Be careful not to overcook the shrimp as they can get quite rubbery.

Serves 4

cohobbolopot

This elegant and festive rice cook-up is a pungent mixture of luxurious ingredients and is ideal for entertaining. If needed, the preparation of the rice, vegetables, etc. can be done well ahead of time. The actual cooking, just before serving, takes only 15-25 minutes. This dish is also worth trying with pasta such as penne or rotini instead of rice.

1lb/500g tomatoes (4-5 medium)
Salt and pepper to taste
1 tablespoon olive oil
2 cups 16floz/500ml rice
4 cups 32floz/1l water
1/2 chicken stock cube
1 tablespoon turmeric powder or 2 tablespoons fresh turmeric, peeled and finely chopped
1/2 teaspoon salt

3 tablespoons chilli oil (if not available use any oil and a little red pepper sauce to taste)
1 medium onion, finely chopped
1/2 teaspoon ground clove
1lb/500g shrimp
1/2lb/250g ham, cut in chunks
1/2 6oz/180g garlic sausage, sliced
2-3 sweet peppers, multi-coloured if possible, cut in 1"/2cm chunks

3 sticks celery, cut in 1"/2cm chunks
4 medium onions, coarsely chopped
2 tablespoons garlic/ 4-6 cloves, finely chopped
1 tablespoon fresh thyme leaves or 1 teaspoon dried thyme
Handful of parsley, finely chopped
Few sprigs of basil, finely chopped
1/2 cup/12 black olives
1/2 cup/12 green olives

1. Preheat the oven to 350F, 180C or Gas Mark 4.
2. Brush a baking sheet with a tablespoon of olive oil and sprinkle with salt. Cut the tomatoes into thick slices, place on the baking sheet, flipping them over so the oil and salt are on both sides of the slices. Bake for 30 minutes.
3. Put the water, stock cube, turmeric, salt, 1 tablespoon of chilli oil, finely chopped onion and clove onto boil at a high heat in a medium saucepan. Place the rice in a large bowl full of water and wash between your hands. Drain and add to the saucepan. When the water and rice are boiling, cover tightly and reduce the heat to low, cooking until all the water has been absorbed (15-20 minutes).
4. Mix the roasted tomatoes into the cooked rice.
5. If using shrimp with the shell on, shell and clean them, removing the back vein and washing any dirt out. Marinate in 1/2 cup milk.

6. Prepare the ham, garlic sausage, celery, onion, garlic, sweet pepper, parsley and basil.
7. Heat 2 tablespoons chilli oil, sauté the onion. Once beginning to brown, add the ham, shrimp, garlic and garlic sausage. Continue to sauté for about 5 minutes and add the rice, sweet peppers, celery, olives, fresh thyme, basil and parsley. Toss until heated through and serve.

Serves 6

chicken curry

With its colourful array of condiments this is excellent party fare. For simply a healthy evening meal, choose a reduced selection of condiments.

4 chicken breasts or 2 breasts and 4 thighs (with skin and bone)

Stock
5 cups 40floz/1.2l water
Large sprigs of thyme, parsley and marjoram
Celery leaves or a stick of celery
1-2 whole, green topped spring onions
1 tablespoon black peppercorns
1 onion, roughly chopped
1 small head of garlic cut in
half crossways
1 chicken stock cube

Curry Sauce
1 tablespoon olive oil
1 onion finely chopped
1 tablespoon garlic finely chopped
1/2 cup/7 tablespoons curry powder
2 cups 16-24floz/500-700ml stock
5 cardamom pods, whole
1 cups 16floz/500ml unsweetened coconut milk (Coconut milk powder mixed with boiling water works well)
2 bay leaves
1 teaspoon ground cumin
1 teaspoon ground ginger
Salt to taste

1. Wash the chicken parts and remove any excess fat. Do not remove the skin yet, since it gives the stock a good flavour. Place the chicken and all the stock ingredients in a pan and bring to the boil. Reduce heat and simmer for about 1/2 hour. Strain off the stock and reserve. Set aside the chicken to cool.
2. In a medium to large saucepan, sauté the onions and curry powder for a couple of minutes. Add the garlic and sauté for a short while longer.
3. Pour in 2 cups of the reserved stock, cardamom pods, coconut milk, bay leaves and cumin. Simmer on a medium heat for about 10 minutes.
4. Remove the chicken from the bones, discard the skin and cut up into large bite size pieces.

5. Once the curry sauce is a nice creamy consistency, taste and add salt and more stock if necessary. Add the chicken and simmer for a further 10-15 minutes. Be careful to stir as little as possible so the chicken remains in nice pieces. Remove the 5 cardamom pods if possible.
6. Serve with hot white rice (page 66) and condiments listed overleaf.

Serves 4-6

shrimp curry/curry condiments

Curry Shrimp: Although it is so easy to use ready cooked shrimp, raw shrimp are recommended since they take up the curry flavour much more. Be very careful, however, not to overcook them as they can quickly become rubbery. If you want to prepare the dish ahead of time, reheat it for just a short while, as the overcooking can of course occur then as well.

Curry Condiments: For a party you can serve all of the suggestions but for a family meal, choose 5 or 6 that your family would enjoy.

4 servings uncooked shrimp (2lbs/1kg with the shell on, 1.5lbs/750g shelled)
1 cup 8floz/250ml milk
1/2 cup curry powder
2 tablespoon garlic finely chopped
1 tablespoon finely chopped ginger
1 tablespoon oil
2 cups 16floz/500ml coconut milk, unsweetened (Coconut milk powder mixed with boiling water works well)
1/2 cup 8floz/250ml fish stock made from 1/4 stock cube)
1 bay leaf
 Garnish: Fresh coriander, red, green and yellow sweet pepper (optional)

Curry Condiments
Mango chutney – page 10
Pumpkin
Eggplant choka
Onion and sweet pepper rings mixed with natural yogurt
Chopped cucumber with a little natural yogurt, salt and a little lime juice (may be mixed with finely chopped fresh mint)
Chopped tomato with a couple of drops of balsamic vinegar and olive oil mixed with finely chopped fresh coriander
Grated coconut
Chopped peanuts
Fried poppadums

Chopped fresh mango
Sliced bananas
Chopped hard-boiled eggs
Dal puri roti skins
Okras creole
Fried plantain

1. Shell, de-vein and wash shrimp. Leave to soak in 1/2 cup milk.
2. Heat oil and sauté curry powder for a few minutes. Then add garlic, coconut milk, 1/2 of the milk, ginger, fish stock and bay leaf.
3. Simmer for about 1/2 hour until well cooked and thickened. If necessary, thicken with a tablespoon of softened butter mixed into a paste with a tablespoon of flour.
4. Add the shrimp and simmer for 5 minutes just before serving.

trini pumpkin/eggplant choka

Here are two delicious recipes of vegetables cooked in their own juices. This preserves the water soluble vitamins and the flavours.

Trini Pumpkin
1lb/500g pumpkin, peeled and diced
1 medium onion, finely chopped
1 tablespoon or 3 cloves garlic, finely chopped
1 tablespoon oil
1 teaspoon light brown sugar
Salt and pepper to taste

1. Sauté the onion and garlic in the oil until they begin to brown.
2. Add diced pumpkin, onion and garlic and cover firmly. Reduce to a medium low heat and allow to steam until pumpkin is soft enough to mash with a spoon.
3. Add a teaspoon of sugar and season to taste with salt and pepper.

Eggplant Choka
1 large eggplant (augbergine, bolangere, melongene)
3 cloves garlic
1 tablespoon oil
A thumbnail piece of green hot pepper, very finely chopped
Salt

1. Pierce the eggplant in three places and insert three cloves of garlic.
2. Roast until the eggplant is soft (15-25 minutes). Choka means roasted. This can be done over a barbecue, an open fire, a gas ring or as a last resort in the oven at 350F, 180C Gas Mark 4.
3. Cut in half and scoop out the pulp. Mash with the oil and hot pepper and season to taste with salt. Serve hot.

fried fish or chicken caribbean style

Caribbean offerings of fried fish and chicken are almost always exceptionally delicious. Three reasons for this are: the fish and chicken are soaked in lime, salt, and water during preparation; they are then marinated or stuffed with savoury Caribbean seasonings; and they are fried in soft, home-seasoned breadcrumbs.

Fish fillets or chicken parts to serve 4
2 limes (use one if they are large and juicy)
2 teaspoons salt
2 tablespoons Caribbean seasoning (page 6)
I egg
I cup 5oz/155g extra fine breadcrumbs
I cup 5oz/155g flour
Salt and white pepper to taste
I teaspoon paprika
I teaspoon chicken or fish multi purpose seasoning (optional)

Oil for frying (Canola or Olive are reputedly healthier)

Salt Breads
Fried fish is often sold sandwiched in a soft, but chewy white bread bun and referred to as a fish cutter.

1. Squeeze the limes into a bowl with 3/4 cup of water, add the salt and place the fish or chicken to soak for about 1/2 hour. Remove the fish or chicken, rinse and pat dry.
2. Whisk the egg in a medium bowl with some salt and white pepper and if you are doing fish, the seasoning. Put the fish into the egg and seasoning mixture.
   If you are doing chicken, make a couple of incisions in each piece, insert some seasoning and place in the egg. It is best if the fish or chicken is allowed to sit in the egg for an hour or so to allow the flavours to permeate.
3. Mix the flour, breadcrumbs, white pepper, paprika and a little salt. This is one of those occasions when you can add various seasonings out of your kitchen cupboard like fish and chicken magic, onion and garlic powder, dried herbs or whatever takes your fancy.

4. Heat very shallow oil for fish and slightly deeper for chicken, in a large frying pan over a medium/high heat. Shake off excess egg, coat in the breadcrumb mixture, shake again and place in the oil when it is hot enough (It should sizzle slightly when the item is placed in it). Fry the fish over the medium/high heat for a couple of minutes on each side. Fish needs very little cooking and is overcooked very easily. If frying flying fish place it skin side up first. Fry chicken over a medium/low heat to allow it to cook through without burning or getting too dark (10-15 minutes on each side depending on how large the piece of chicken is).
5. Drain on absorbent paper and place on a warm dish.

Serves 4

chicken creole/creole fish

Chicken Creole: This easy and nutritious chicken dish is delicious when served with steamed white rice and green vegetables such as string beans. You can use either chicken parts with skin and bones which give a better flavour to the sauce or chicken strips or fillets which are healthier.

Creole Fish: Just about any fish can be used for this recipe:- small whole snappers, rolled boned flying fish, boneless fillets of fish such as wahoo, barracuda, grouper or mahi mahi. This goes well with most starches and vegetables especially cou cou, ground provisions and rice.

Chicken Creole

4 servings of chicken, trimmed of any
excess fat, washed and dried
I cup 5oz/155g flour
I tablespoon freshly ground black
pepper
I teaspoon salt
I teaspoon paprika
1/4 cup 2floz/125ml olive oil
I large can 32oz/960ml tomatoes or
11/2lbs/750g fresh tomatoes, peeled
12 small or 4 medium onions, chopped
2 tablespoons garlic, finely chopped
I cup 8floz/250ml chicken stock (can be
made with a chicken stock cube)
Large handful fresh parsley, chopped
1/2 cup/small handful fresh basil, chopped
Red pepper sauce to taste

Creole Fish

4 servings fresh fish
(whole fish or fillets)
2 limes
I teaspoon salt
2 tablespoons olive oil
2 tablespoons Caribbean seasoning
8 medium or 12 small onions, cut in rings
I large or 2 medium sweet peppers cut
in rings (multi-coloured, if preferred)
I celery stick, chopped
2 tablespoons garlic, finely chopped
Bunch of fresh herbs, (parsley, thyme,
marjoram, basil, scallions/spring onions)
Pepper sauce to taste
I large can 32floz/960ml tomatoes
chopped or 11/2lbs/750g fresh tomatoes,
scalded, peeled and chopped
Worcestershire sauce
I 1/2 cups 12floz/360ml fish stock

For the fish stock, either dissolve a fish stock cube in boiling water or if you have any fish bones or trimmings, make a fresh fish stock for this recipe by boiling them for 10
minutes along with salt, pepper, a bunch of fresh herbs, a thumbnail of fresh hot pepper and a piece of onion.
Garnish: Sprigs of fresh basil or parsley and slices of lime

1. Mix the flour, salt, pepper and paprika and coat the chicken in this mixture.
2. Heat the olive oil in a large frying pan and lightly brown the chicken pieces on a medium heat. Remove and set aside.
3. Coarsely chop the can of tomatoes.
4. Pour off some of the oil from the pan and saute the onions until light brown. Add the garlic, tomatoes, stock, parsley, basil, pepper sauce and browned chicken.
5. Simmer uncovered for about 1/2 hour, replacing liquid as necessary.

1. Wash the fish and soak in the water, salt and the juice of one lime for 20-30 minutes.
2. Drain and rinse the fish, coat well in the Caribbean seasoning and allow to marinate
3. Meanwhile, heat the olive oil in a large frying pan and sauté the onions until beginning to brown. Add the garlic and sweet pepper rings and sauté for another minute. Add the tomatoes, a tablespoon of lime juice, pepper sauce and worcestershire sauce to taste, finely chopped fresh herbs and the fish stock.

4. Cover the pan and allow the sauce to simmer for 20 minutes.
5. Add the fish and continue to simmer covered, for 10-15 minutes, depending on the thickness of the fish fillets and serve.

big soup

This is a very filling and healthy soup. It is fat-free, easy to digest and full of nutrients. Lamb, crab or fish can be used instead of chicken. A wide variety of other vegetables can be included such as green bananas, yams, okras, eddoes, breadfruit, mushrooms, corn, leeks, squash and zucchini to name a few. Add the slower cooking vegetables such as yams and green bananas first and the faster cooking vegetables such as mushrooms, okras and zucchini for a few minutes just before the soup is finished cooking.

1lb/500g chicken parts with skin and bones

Stock
9 cups 45floz/1.35l of water
1-2 large sprigs of thyme, parsley and marjoram
Celery leaves or a stick of celery
1-2 whole, green topped spring onions
Ground black pepper to taste
1 onion
2 cloves garlic
1 chicken stock cube

Vegetables
3 medium English potatoes, cut in chunks
1 medium sweet potato, cut in chunks
3 carrots cut in 1" pieces
1 small onion, finely chopped
A sprig of thyme and marjoram whole
2 spring onions (scallions) whole
1lb/500g pumpkin, cut in chunks
1 stick celery, chopped
1 medium sweet pepper, cubed
2 cups 10oz/315g cauliflower, broken into florets
2 cups 10oz/315g broccoli florets

1. Wash the chicken parts and remove any excess fat. Do not remove the skin yet since it gives the stock a good flavour. Place the chicken and all the stock ingredients in a large saucepan. Once brought to the boil, reduce heat to medium and simmer for about 1/2 hour.
2. Remove chicken and strain the stock. It should yield about eight cups stock.
3. Put the stock, onion, fresh herbs, spring onions, English and sweet potatoes, and carrots into the saucepan, bring to the boil and then simmer for about 10 minutes.
4. Cut up the chicken into bite size pieces.
5. Add the pumpkin, celery, sweet pepper, cauliflower, chicken and broccoli and continue to simmer for another 5 or 10 minutes until the vegetables are cooked.

6. Remove the spring onions and sprigs of herbs before serving. Add salt and pepper to taste.

Serves 4 as a main course and 8 as an appetizer.

chicken chow mein

Introduced to the Caribbean by the large numbers of chinese immigrants that came to Trinidad in the mid 1800's, Chow Mein is now established as an everyday dish in many islands. This healthy, light and easy one-pot meal tastes best when the noodles are cooked in the chicken stock. However, if you wish to eliminate the stock section of this recipe, you may instead cook the noodles with a chicken stock cube in the water. You will then have to cut up the chicken raw and sauté it along with the onions.

4 chicken breasts with skin and bones or
2 breasts and 4 thighs on the bone

Stock
8 cups 40floz/1.2l water
Large sprigs of thyme, parsley and marjoram
Celery leaves or a stick of celery
1-2 whole, green topped spring onions
1 tablespoon black peppercorns
1 medium onion
1/2 small head of garlic cut in half crossways

1 chicken stock cube
1/2 teaspoon pepper sauce or
1/4 fresh pepper
2 tablespoons soy sauce

10oz/315g oriental egg noodles

1 teaspoon sesame oil
1 tablespoon oil
4 medium onions, finely chopped
1 tablespoon garlic, finely chopped
1 cup 6oz/185g carrots, julienne (slivers)

1 1/2 cups 8oz/250g snow peas
3/4 cup 4oz/125g sweet pepper, mulit-coloured if possible, julienne (slivers)
1/2 cup 3oz/90g spring onions, chopped
2 cups 12oz/375g brocolli cut into florets
8oz/250g tin water chestnuts, sliced
14oz/440g tin baby sweet corn on the cob, chopped
2 tablespoons soy sauce
1 teaspoon red pepper sauce

1. Place all the stock ingredients and the chicken in a large saucepan. Bring to the boil and then simmer on a medium heat for about 1/2 hour.
2. Strain the stock into a large saucepan, reserving the chicken. Bring the stock back to the boil, add the noodles and cook until tender but still with a little bite (3-5 minutes – Chinese egg noodles cook in about half the time of pasta).
3. Strain and cool the noodles on a large platter or pan so as to dry them out. The noodes sometimes stick together as they cool but you can separate them by shaking with an oily fork.
4. Meanwhile, remove the chicken skin, de-bone, cut into bite size pieces and set aside.

5. In a large frying pan or wok heat the two oils and sauté the onions until they begin to brown and then add the garlic, sweet peppers, carrots, brocolli, water chestnuts, snow peas and sweet corn. Sauté the vegetables for a few minutes, add the cooked noodles and stir-fry for a couple more minutes, being careful not to mush the noodles.
6. Lastly, add the chicken and spring onions. Sauté until chicken is heated through. Season to taste with soya sauce and pepper sauce and serve.

Serves 6

chicken pelau

Pelau is actually derived from Spanish Paella, and many people here in the Caribbean view it as a cook-up of whatever is in the fridge or the larder just before shopping day. The recipe provided here may act as the basis from which to create your own specialized "cook-up", for one may add vegetables such a pigeon peas, tomatoes, carrots, beets, celery sticks, sweet pepper, beans, etc. If adding a cup of fresh pigeon peas, cook them first along with the chicken.

4 chicken breasts or 2 breasts and 4 thighs (with skin and bones)

Stock
8 cups 40floz/1.2l water
Large sprigs of thyme, parsley and marjoram
Celery leaves or a stick of celery
1-2 whole, green topped spring onions
1 tablespoon black or multi-coloured peppercorns
1 onion
1/2 small head of garlic halved crossways

1 chicken stock cube
1/2 fresh hot pepper, seeds removed
2 tablespoons soy sauce

Pelau
3 cups 24floz/750ml rice
1 tablespoon olive oil
4 medium onions finely chopped
6 rashers streaky bacon, cut up
3 tablespoons sugar

Garnish: 12 pimento stuffed olives, sprigs of parsley, red sweet pepper

1. Place all the stock ingredients and the chicken in a large saucepan. Bring to the boil and then simmer on a medium heat for about 1/2 hour.
2. Remove the chicken, cool, remove the skin, de-bone and cut into bite size pieces. Strain and reserve the stock.
3. Place the rice in a large bowl of water, wash thoroughly and drain well.
4. Place the olive oil and sugar in a large saucepan and sauté until the sugar has turned dark brown. Add the bacon and onions and continue to sauté until the onion begins to brown and the bacon is cooked, but not crispy. Add the washed raw rice and fry for a few minutes, stirring periodically. Add the chicken, 6 cups of stock and any vegetables you like. Bring to the boil, cover tightly and reduce the heat to low.

5. Cook until all the liquid is completely absorbed. Then dish, garnish and serve. Serve mango chutney on the side.

Serves 4-6

pudding & souse

Steeped in tradition, souse in the Caribbean is usually made with pigs head and trotters. However pork chops, with the skin on, are easier to find and cook and make an excellent, less fatty, very tasty souse. Pudding, made with sweet potato, is generally stuffed into pigs intestine and steamed as black or white pudding, but is quite nice steamed in a pudding bowl. Pudding and souse are made and sold throughout Barbados every Saturday. This recipe gives a simple version that is easily be prepared at home. Although generally eaten as a main course dish with pudding and pickled breadfruit, soused pork chops make an excellent canapé or appetizer.

Soused Pork Chops

5 pork chops with the skin on
3 cups 24floz/725ml water
1 onion
Bunch of herbs
Pepper sauce, black pepper and salt to taste
1 chicken stock cube (optional)
2 cups/3-6 peeled cucumbers, finely chopped – choose cucumbers with as few seeds as possible

1/2 cup/2 medium onions, finely chopped
1/3 cup lime juice (juice of 2 or 3 limes, enough to give the pickle a good twang)
1 teaspoon salt
Small bunch parsley, finely chopped
1 teaspoon hot pepper, very finely chopped or 1/2 teaspoon red pepper sauce – adjust to taste
To garnish: Sweet pepper rings and parsley

1. Wash the pork chops and place in a saucepan with water, onion, herbs, pepper sauce, pepper, salt and stock cube if using. It is said, "de sweeter de souse water, de sweeter de souse". Bring to the boil and simmer for about 1/2 hour or until the pork is tender.
2. Meanwhile, prepare the pickle of cucumber, onion, lime juice, salt, parsley and hot pepper and refrigerate.
3. When the pork chops are cooked, strain off the liquid, reserving a little and allow to cool. Cut into strips crossways (each slice should have skin, fat and meat and be about 1/8/3mm inch thick.)
4. Add the sliced pork to the pickle and mix well. Souse should be eaten within 6 or 8 hours of being made, as the pickle tends to deteriorate after that.
5. Serve garnished with parsley and sweet pepper rings.

Pudding

2-3 lbs1-1.5kg sweet potato
2-3 green topped spring onions, finely chopped
2 tablespoons fresh thyme leaves
2 tablespoons fresh marjoram
4 tablespoons butter
1 tablespoon light brown sugar
1/2 teaspoon powdered cloves
1 very hot bonnet or chilli pepper
1-2 tablespoons flour (optional)

1. Peel and grate the sweet potato on the very fine, but bumpy side of the grater that gives the finest texture.
2. Mix the grated sweet potato with the herbs, butter, sugar, cloves and minced hot pepper. Add enough hot water to make a soft but not runny texture. Add 1 or 2 tablespoons flour if the sweet potatoes are not very starchy and the mixture is too runny.
3. Pour into a pyrex or metal steaming bowl and steam over boiling water for an hour or until an inserted scewer comes out clean.

Conch, pictured on the facing page, also makes a delicious souse. See page 26.

stewed down chops

This is hearty fare for lunch or dinner that is popular with all ages. Delicious served with mashed potatoes or rice and steamed vegetables.

4 servings pork chops (preferably with the skin on) or lamb chops
2 tablespoons olive oil
8 medium onions, quartered and sliced
1 cup/2 sweet peppers, diced
2 tablespoons garlic, finely chopped
1 teaspoon grated nutmeg
2 tablespoons fresh thyme or
1 tablespoon dried thyme
Pepper sauce to taste
A few dashes of worcestershire sauce

A few dashes of Angostura bitters
2 cups 14floz/425ml can peeled tomatoes, diced
2 cups 16floz/500ml water

1. Rub salt on to the pork chops and leave for 10 minutes. Wash and pat dry.
2. Heat the oil in a large frying pan and brown the chops on both sides over a medium to high heat (about 10 mins). Remove the chops from the pan and set aside.
3. Sauté the onions until beginning to brown, add the garlic and sweet peppers and sauté for a further couple of minutes. Add the tomatoes, nutmeg, thyme, worcestershire sauce, Angostura bitters, water and replace the pork chops.
4. Cover and simmer over a low heat until the chops are tender (1-2 hours) Add more water during cooking if necessary.

Serves 4

roast pork

Roast Pork: Is especially delicious in the Caribbean. Pigs played an important sociological role in the region, reared and slaughtered in back yards, they supplemented the meagre wages of the workers and saw many a family through hard times or financed their betterment. The revered leg and shoulder roasts are the prized parts of the pig. Incisions are made into the pork and filled with Caribbean Seasoning. The skin is scored into tiny squares and you can usually rely on it becoming delicious crispy crackling.

Gravy: The quantities in this recipe apply to a medium roast. If you are cooking a large roast, multiply it or with a very small roast, half it.

Roast of pork
Caribbean seasoning page 6
Limes
Salt
Yellow American mustard
Water

Gravy
2 tablespoons pork fat or olive oil, if you prefer
2 tablespoons flour (Use more if you like a thick gravy and less if you like a thin gravy)
3 cups liquid from the roasting tin
Worcestershire sauce to taste
Salt and freshly ground black pepper
1 tablespoon onion powder
1 teaspoon gravy browning

Rub the fresh or frozen pork in plenty of salt, place in plastic bag and put in the bottom of the fridge overnight or for up to 2 days. Wash the pork, pat dry and coat in lime juice and salt. Using a long sharp knife, make deep incisions strategically in the joint and push in Caribbean seasoning. Score the skin into 1" squares. Lather each piece of skin with plenty of yellow "hot dog" mustard. (The mustard and its flavour completely disappears and gives delicious crispy crackling.) Place in an open roasting pan with 2" of water. Pork is suitable for either fast or slow roasting. A larger joint is better cooked in a slower oven so that the outside doesn't overcook before the center is well done. Pork should always be eaten well cooked, rare pork can contain harmful bacteria that may cause severe illness. In order to have a delicious gravy stock, keep the liquid topped up in the roasting pan during cooking. Do not cover during roasting.

Fast Roasting - Small to medium roasts. 25 minutes per lb/500g, 25 minutes over Preheat the oven to hot 450F, 220C or Gas Mark 6. After 20 minutes of cooking, lower to moderately hot, 400F, 200C or Gas Mark 5.

Slow Roasting - Medium to large roasts 35 minutes per lb/500g, 35 minutes over. Preheat oven at moderate 350F, 180C or Gas Mark 4 and keep at this setting.

The pork is well cooked when it is skewered right to the center of the roast and only a minimal amount of clear liquid comes out. Remove the roast from the pan and set aside to cool. Pour the dripping and liquid out of the roasting pan into a jug. (Separator jug if possible)

1. If you have a separator jug this is ideal as it allows you to easily separate all the fat from the liquid out of the roasting tin. If not just spoon it off , and place two tablespoons of the fat in a medium saucepan.
2. Heat the fat or oil and add the flour. Cook the flour for a couple of minutes, stirring until it's brown.
3. Add the stock, gradually. Each time it comes to the boil, remove the pan from the heat and beat with a wooden spoon until well blended.
4. When all the liquid has been added, continue to simmer on a medium heat, stirring occasionally and add the gravy browning. Season to taste with worcestershire sauce, salt and freshly ground black pepper and onion powder.

glazed ham with hot sorrel sauce

This traditional Christmas fare is ideal for a buffet at any time of the year. It can also be made with a small picnic ham and served as a family treat, carving the hot ham at the table. The earthy and tangy taste of sorrel goes perfectly with ham, but if this juice is unavailable, supplement with cider or pineapple juice. Fresh sorrel is only sold around Christmas but dried sorrel is available throughout the year so you can make the sorrel drink by simply steeping the dried sepals in boiling water with some cloves, cinnamon and fresh ginger and adding sugar to taste.

1 pre-cooked ham approx 8lb /4kg
2 1/2 cups 20floz/600ml sorrel drink
1/2 cup 6oz/185g light brown sugar
1 teaspoon ground cloves
1 teaspoon ground cinnamon
The rind and juice of 1 lime
1 cup 5oz/155g raisins/sultanas
3 teaspoons English hot dry mustard
2 tablespoons cornstarch or arrowroot
2 tablespoons cold water

1. Remove most of the fat from the ham, leaving a thin layer to seal the ham. Place ham, fat side up in a roasting pan.
2. Combine sorrel, half of the brown sugar (1/4 cup), powdered clove and cinnamon, 2 teaspoons English hot dry mustard, (the third teaspoon for the ham glaze and lime rind and juice and pour over the ham. If you don't have a rind paring tool use the small side of a grater).
3. Cover with baking tin lid or foil and bake the ham at 325F, 160C or Gas Mark 3, basting frequently, for 1 1/2 hours.
4. Add raisins and bake for 1/2 hour longer.
5. Remove the ham from the oven and pour off the pan liquid with raisins. Combine remaining 1/2 (1/4 cup) of the brown sugar with dry mustard and press onto ham. 1/2 hour before you are going to eat, bake the ham uncovered for about 30 minutes longer in a hotter oven 400F, 200C or Gas Mark 5, to set the glaze.
6. To make the hot sorrel sauce skim off the fat from the pan juices. This can be done quickly using a fat separator or simply by spooning off the top. Mix the cornstarch or arrowroot flour with 2 tablespoons water. Place the pan juices including the raisins into a medium saucepan, add in the cornstarch mixture, bring to the boil and then reduce the heat to simmer, stirring constantly until it is thickened. Set aside to reheat when ready to serve.
7. After the ham has baked with the glaze, heat the sorrel sauce and pour a small amount over the ham and serving the rest in a gravy boat along with yellow pepper sauce and English hot mustard.

pepperpot

This method of cooking and preserving meat was introduced by the indigenous Amerindian population of Guyana, and has become that country's national dish. Cassareep is a thick, black preservative sauce made from Cassava, a root crop. This hot, spicy, slightly sweet, almost black stew is delicious served with mashed sweet potato or steamed rice. The traditional businessmen's clubs in the Caribbean islands' capitals such as Bridgetown and Georgetown were said to have had the same pepperpot on the go for years, continuously adding ingredients and boiling it up daily. Today it is made during holidays and at festive occasions.

3lbs/1.5kg beef oxtails
4lb/2kg pork hocks or beef
1.5lb/750g salted pork or beef
3-4lbs/750-1000g chicken parts or a
whole chicken cut up
4-6 scotch bonnet or chilli peppers (As
hot as possible)
2 cups 16floz/500ml cassareep
Salt to taste

1. Boil the beef oxtails and salted beef or pork for 1-2 hours. Pork skin gives a good flavour and texture to pepperpot so do not remove it and include some salted pig tails in the salt pork, if possible.
2. Cut up the chicken and beef or pork and fry in a little oil. Taste the liquid with the salt meat and oxtails and dilute if it is too salty by pouring off some liquid and adding water. Add the browned chicken, beef or pork to the oxtails etc.
3. Add the cassareep and salt to taste. Tie up the peppers in a small muslin bag. You can use a square of thin cloth and a piece of string. Stick the peppers through the cloth of the bag with a fork to release all the pepper juices and place in the saucepan. Simmer on a low heat until the meat is tender (About 4 hours).
4. Hot water and cassareep may be added when more sauce is needed, and more meat can be fried and added. Pepperpot can be kept without refrigeration, but it must be boiled up everyday for 1/2 hour or more and kept covered. If the pepperpot is not being eaten on a daily basis it is best to freeze the pepperpot after the initial serving. The daily boiling which is required, overcooks the meats making them hard and very stringy.

Serves 20-25

Pepperpot Rules
1. Vegetables or starchy foods should not be added to pepperpot. This pepperpot should not be confused with the thick vegetable pepperpot soup served in the northern Caribbean.
2. Lamb should never be added to pepperpot.
3. If not frozen, pepperpot must be kept covered and boiled up everyday for 1/2 hour, if kept out of the fridge.

delicious beef stew

The islands are famous for tasty stews and their secret is the pungent combination of pepper sauce and fresh herbs. Beetroots, carrots and the delicious nutty taste of green bananas lightens up the traditionally spicy Caribbean beef stew but the recipe is still delicious without them. Green bananas are loaded with vitamins and minerals most notably iron. Serve with rice.

1 tablespoon vegetable oil
1 1/2 lbs/750g stew beef
1 medium onion
2 tablespoons garlic, finely chopped
2 tablespoons Caribbean seasoning (optional)
6 cups 48floz/1.5l water
1/2 tablespoon gravy browning
1/2 teaspoon pepper sauce
1/2 stick celery
1 sprig fresh thyme (1/2 teaspoon dried)

1 sprig fresh marjoram (1/2 teaspoon dried)
1 beef stock cube
1 tablespoon butter (optional)
3 tablespoons flour (optional)
1 bay leaf
1/2 lb/250g carrots
1 large/2 small beetroot
Salt and freshly ground pepper to taste
1 lb/500g green bananas peeled (optional)

1. Wash beef, pat dry and cut into very small cubes. Place in a bowl with the onion, garlic, pepper sauce, seasoning (optional),celery, herbs and beef cube. Mix well and leave to marinate if possible.
2. Heat the oil and sauté beef for a few minutes, add water and the gravy browning and bring to the boil. Reduce heat to medium and simmer until tender (40 minutes to an hour depending on the quality of the beef).
3. Mix butter and flour into a paste and add to the stew to thicken, stirring until well blended. Add salt and pepper, bayleaf, carrots, beetroot and green bananas (if including) and simmer until the vegetables are tender (about 15 mins).

Serves 4-6

patties

Hot and spicy meat filled patties are made throughout the Caribbean in various forms, but the Jamaican patty is probably the most popular. The recipe below contains potato, which helps to thicken the filling. However, if you prefer to leave this ingredient out, then thicken with flour. Other vegetables may also be added to make a more nutritious, light meal. Note that the filling needs to be cold when making the patties, so it has to be made ahead of time and refrigerated.

Filling
2 tablespoons oil
1 cup/3 medium onions, finely chopped
1 tablespoon garlic, finely chopped
12oz/360g minced beef
12floz/360ml medium tin peeled tomatoes (or 1 cup 8floz/250ml chunky pasta sauce)
1 beef stock cube
1 teaspoon dried thyme or 1 tablespoon fresh thyme leaves
1/4 cup/2-3 chopped green topped spring onions/scallions

Freshly ground peppercorns and salt
1 cup 8floz/250ml water
A few dashes of worcestershire sauce
Red or yellow pepper sauce or fresh hot pepper to taste
2 cups/4 medium diced raw potato

Pastry
5oz/155g lard
5oz/155g margarine
3 cups 1lb/500g flour
1 teaspoon salt
1 tablespoon curry powder or English

hot mustard powder
1/4-1 cup 8floz/250ml very cold water. Different flours require very different amounts of water. In the Caribbean the flour tends to require the full cup. The golden rule is simply, put enough water to make the pastry hold together well. A pastry with dry cracks is difficult to role out.
1 egg for brushing the patties.

Makes 20-24 patties

Filling
1. The filling for these patties has to be cold, so it needs to be made ahead of time and refrigerated.
2. Heat the oil in a medium saucepan, and sauté the onions. As they begin to soften and brown slightly add the garlic, scallions and minced beef. Continue to sauté for a few minutes.
3. Cut up the tinned tomatoes and add to the beef along with the crumbled beef stock cube, thyme, worcestershire sauce, pepper sauce to taste, water, potatoes, black pepper and salt to taste.
4. Simmer over a low to medium heat until the liquid is almost all evaporated.
5. Cool and refrigerate.

Pastry
1. To make pastry in a food processor, the lard and margarine should be very cold. This can be a challenge in the warm Caribbean. Either store them in your freezer and shred them into the flour or if they are in the fridge, cut them up into fingernail size piece and harden in the freezer for 10 minutes.
2. Sieve the flour, salt and curry powder or mustard into a food processor. Add the margarine and lard. Process for 30 seconds. Do not over process.
3. Tip into a bowl, pour in the very cold water and mix with a flat knife.
4. Knead gently with the tips of your fingers, just enough to form a ball. Wrap in waxed paper and refrigerate for 1/2 hour.

Patties
1. Preheat the oven at 375F, 190C or Gas Mark 4.
2. Roll out the pastry. Cut in circles 3-4" in diameter. Place the meat in the centre. Wet the edge of the circle with water and fold over to form a crescent. Press down with a fork or your fingers to seal the patty. Cut or stick a little hole in the top of the patty to let the steam out when it is baking.
3. Place on a well greased baking sheet and brush with beaten egg. Bake for 25-30 minutes.
4. If you are preparing them well before serving or freezing them, you can cook them for 15-20 minutes and finish baking them just before serving.

mangopineapplelime

sweetness

mango mousse with passion fruit sauce

It is the stiffly beaten egg white in this mousse that makes it so light and fluffy and, as with any mousse, you can use it to make a cold soufflé, if so desired. This may be done by surrounding a smaller soufflé dish with a couple of layers of wax paper, secured with string and pouring the mousse about two inches/5cm above the top of the dish, held in by the paper. When set, remove the paper and decorate the sides with grated coconut and the top with cream and mango slices.

Mango Mousse
3lbs/1.5kg ripe mango, peeled and flesh
cut off seed to give 4-5 cups diced
mango
1 1/2 cups 12floz/360ml whipping cream
2 egg whites
1-2 tablespoons lime juice to taste
1/2-1 cup 4-8oz/125-250g sugar

2 packages gelatin
1/2 cup 4floz/125ml hot water
Garnish: 1/2 cup 4floz/120floz whipping
cream, 6-7 slices mango and a slice lime

Passion Fruit Sauce
4 passion fruit
4 tablespoons light brown sugar
1/2 cup 4floz/125ml water

Mango Mousse
1. Purée the mango in a food processor or blender to yield 3 cups mango purée. Some mangos are very stringy and if this is the case, strain the purée.
2. Pour the cream into a small mixing bowl and place in the freezer for 10 minutes. Cream needs to be very cold to whip successfully.
3. Beat the egg white in a completely dry and clean mixing bowl until stiff.
4. Beat the cream until it stands in peaks and place in the fridge.
5. Soften the gelatin in a little cold water and dissolve the gelatin and the sugar in the 1/2 cup of hot water. Add to the mango puree in a mixing bowl along with lime juice and sugar to taste. The amount of lime and sugar added depends on both your taste and the acidity of the mangoes used. If the mango is tart enough add no lime juice at all. Fold the egg whites, cream and mango until well blended.
6. Pour into one serving dish or individual serving dishes and set in the refrigerator. (About 6 hours)

7. Just before serving, garnish with whipped cream, sliced mango and lime. Serves 8

Passion Fruit Sauce
1. Place the sugar and water in a saucepan and boil, stirring until a syrup is formed.
2. Cut the passion fruit in half and scoop out the pulp and seeds.
3. Place pulp and seeds in the hot syrup and allow to steep for 10 minutes.
4. Strain, putting a few seeds back in for style. Chill.
5. Serve on the side.

This sauce is also a drink concentrate. Add soda or water and serve with ice. It is also ideal for making passiontinis (page 12).

How to serve a mango
1. A mango is ripe when you are able to make a small dent with your finger.
2. Place the mango on a chopping board, stem end up.
3. Using a serrated knife, cut off the two flattest sides or cheeks, as close to the seed as possible. Cut off the two remaining sides or strips.
4. Using the tip of the knife blade, cut strips through the mango flesh in each of the slices, being careful not to cut the skin. Cut accross the strips to make squares of mango.
5. Hold each slice and turn it inside out, so that the mango protrudes and serve along with the seed. Ripe mangos, debatably, taste better chilled.

lime cheesecake with ginger crust

Here are two truly excellent cheesecakes. Only the bases require baking while the fillngs are to be refrigerated. Option one is a light yet very creamy and tasty cheesecake, which unfortunately takes quite a long time to prepare. The tangy taste of lime combined with freshly made custard and cream cheese is absolutely delicious, and hence this recipe is well worth its lengthy preparation. Although option two contains a hefty 2 lbs of cream cheese, it has marshmallows instead of eggs and no cream. The best news about option 2, however, is that it is quicker and easier.

Ginger Crust:
11/2 7oz/200g packs digestive biscuits (3 cups crushed)
3/4 cup 6oz/90g melted butter
2 teaspoons grated fresh ginger or ground ginger
1/3 cup 3oz/90g brown sugar
Filling option 1:
1/2 cup 4floz/125ml cream
1 teaspoon vanilla essence
2 tablespoons gelatin (About 2 envelopes)

2 eggs
1/2 cup 4oz/125g caster sugar (for egg yolks)
1/3 cup 3oz/90g caster sugar (for egg whites)
1/3 cup 3floz/100ml water
3 tablespoons fresh lime juice
2/3 cup 5floz/150ml fresh whipping cream
1lb/500g cream cheese (2 8 oz packs)

Filling easy option 2
2 tablespoons gelatin (About 2 envelopes)
1 cup 3floz/100ml water
1/4-1/2 cup sugar
3 tablespoons fresh lime juice
2 cups marshmallows
2lb/1kg cream cheese (4-8 oz packs)
Garnish: Limes, green or yellow as thinly sliced as possible, sliced fresh mango, guava stew or tinned cherry pie filling.

Crust
1. Place the digestive/graham crackers in a food processor and process until crushed (20-40 seconds).
2. Melt the butter in a small saucepan. Add the sugar and ginger and stir until dissolved. Add the biscuit crumbs and mix until thoroughly blended.
3. Put crumbs into a 10" -12" pie dish or spring-form pan and pat down.
4. Bake in a cool preheated oven (Gas mark 2, 140C, 300F), for 15 minutes.
Filling - option 1
1. Heat the single cream in a double boiler with the vanilla essence.
2. Separate the eggs, placing the whites in one medium, very clean and dry mixing bowl and the yolks in another.
3. Beat the yolks with 3/4 cup sugar and pinch salt until thick and creamy. Add to the heated cream and stir with a whisk over the hot water until, a thick and creamy custard is formed (15-20 mins).

4. Soften the gelatin in 1/2 cup water and stir into the hot custard until dissolved. Cool the custard.
5. Mash and soften the cream cheese and blend with the custard and the lime juice.
6. Beat the egg whites with clean and dry beaters until stiff and then gradually add a 1/2 cup caster sugar, beating constantly. Fold this into the custard mixture.
7. Beat the whipping cream until stiff and then fold that into the custard.
8. Fill the crust with this mixture. Chill until set (3-4 hours).
9. Decorate with very thinly sliced limes. This cheesecake tends to have a better texture if it is taken out of the fridge about 1/2 hour before serving.

Filling - option 2
1. Heat the water, sugar and lime juice in a small saucepan. Soften the gelatin in a little cold water. Dissolve in the boiling water.
2. Add the marshmallows and stir until dissolved. Cool until slightly stiff. This process can be speeded up in a freezer.
3. Soften the cream cheese in a food processor and add the galatin mixture. Process until smooth.
4. Pour into the crust and garnish with thinly sliced lime.
5. Chill until set (3-4 hours).

lime meringue pie

This tart lime curd topped with sweet meringue is an explosion of taste and a wonderful end to a meal. You can take a couple of shortcuts such as buying a ready made crust or buying instant lemon meringue pie filling and adding lime juice and brown sugar. If you use brown sugar to make the filling, which some find is much tastier, the colour of the finished curd is a yellowy brown. If this bothers you, add some green and yellow food dye. Meringue pies can be quite troublesome so follow the recipe exactly.

9 Pastry Crust
1 1/2 cups 8oz/250g flour
1/4 cup 2oz/60g butter
1/4 cup 2oz/60g lard
Pinch of salt
2 teaspoons sugar
1/4-1/2 cup 2-4floz/60-125ml iced water

Filling
1/4 cup lime juice
1cup straw sugar
2 cups water
5-6 tablespoons corn flour or arrowroot
1 tablespoon grated lime rind
1oz/30g butter
4 egg yolks
Pinch of salt

Meringue Topping
4 egg whites
1/2 cup 5oz/155g castor sugar
1/2 teaspoon cream of tartar
Garnish:1 twist of lime or pared lime rind

Pastry
1. Measure the butter and lard and place in the freezer.
2. Sieve the flour and place in a food processor along with the salt and sugar. Take the butter and lard out of the freezer and add to the flour in the food processor in small chips. Process for 10-20 seconds to form crumbs.
3. Turn into a bowl and add the iced water gradually, mixing well with a spatula. Use more or less water as necessary in order to get a slightly moist ball of pastry. Try to avoid touching the pastry with your hands in order to keep the mixture as cool as possible.
4. Preheat the oven to 400F, 200C or Gas Mark 5
5. Roll out on a well floured surface, turning the pastry and always rolling in the same direction.
6. Loop the pastry over the rolling pin and place over a 9 67cm pie dish. Flatten into the dish and trim the excess pastry from around the edge. Stick the

bottom of the crust with a fork.
7. Cover the bottom and sides with a piece of waxed paper and a cup of dried beans or peas. Bake blind in the centre of the oven for 10 minutes.

Filling
1. Separate the eggs, being extremely careful not to get any yolk in the whites. It is best to separate each egg into a little bowl so that if you make a slip it doesn t affect all the egg whites.
2. Using the finest side of the grater, grate the outer rind, or zest, off the limes to get 1 tablespoon of grated rind. Then squeeze them until you get 1/4 cup lime juice.
3. Place the water, sugar, and cornstarch or arrowroot in a double boiler, over and not in water. Bring to the boil and reduce the heat to medium /low to allow it to simmer, stirring continuously, until the mixture is thick. Remove from the heat.
4. Whisk the egg yolks until thick and creamy and whisk in a little of the curd.

Stir egg mixture into the rest of the curd, and return to a medium heat for a few minutes, stirring occasionally.
5. Remove from heat and beat in the butter, lime juice and lime rind. Too much lime juice will make the filling runny so if you want a more tart filling increase the lime rind.
6. Stir until cool and place in pastry case.

Meringue Topping
1. Preheat the oven to 325F, 160C or Gas Mark 3. The meringue needs to go directly in the oven after beating.
2. Using the high speed of an electric mixer, whisk the egg whites and cream of tartar until it forms floppy peaks.
3. Continue whisking while gradually adding the white sugar, a teaspoon at a time. Don t overbeat or add extra sugar.
4. Spoon over the top of the pie and spread.
5. Bake for 15-20 minutes or until the meringue is golden. Serve hot or cold.

Serves 8-10

sticky pineapple upside down cake

The pineapple was another fruit that was introduced to the world from the Caribbean, not being taken to Hawaii until the mid 1800's. It was the revered fruit of the fierce Carib Indians after whom the Caribbean is named, and viewed by them as a symbol of hospitality. This version of pineapple upside down cake has a caramel that renders it a very moist dessert. Those with a sweet tooth may like to double the Caramel sauce ingredients (butter, sugar and golden syrup) and reserve half of it to serve on the side.

To line the tin
1/2 cup 4oz/125g sugar
2oz/60g butter
1/4 cup 2floz/60ml golden sugar
1/4 cup water
1 large tin 20oz/567g sliced pineapple
1 lime (optional)
10-15 glace or maraschino cherries
A few stick of angelica (optional)

Cake
6oz/185g butter or margarine
3/4 cup 6oz/185g sugar
2 teaspoons vanilla essence
3 eggs
1/2 cup reserved juice from the tin
1 cup 6oz/185g flour
3 teaspoons baking powder (if using
self-raising flour only use one teaspoon
baking powder)
1/2 teaspoon salt

1. Place the water, sugar, butter and golden syrup. Bring to the boil and simmer one the bottom.
3. Pour the half caramel into the pan and reserve the other half to heat up and pour over just before serving. Put the pineapple slices on top and squeeze a little lime juice on them. This gives a little welcome tartness to the pineapple that contrasts well with the sweet caramel. Reserve the juice from the tin to put in the cake mixture. Decorate with the cherries (and angelica). Set aside.
4. Preheat a moderate oven 325F, 160C or Gas Mark 3.
5. Place all the cake ingredients into a food processor in the order they are listed, sifting the flour, baking powder and salt.
6. Process for 20-25 seconds (no longer). Drop in spoonfuls on top of the pineapples in the pan and spread the mixture carefully. Bake in the centre of the oven for 30-35 minutes or until the cake is golden brown, firm to the touch and an inserted skewer comes out clean.
7. Serve hot or at room temperature.

Serves 8-10

sticky toffee rum date pudding

Britain played an undeniable role in creating the Caribbean we now know, and this pudding recipe is just one of the many colonial legacies that exists within our region today. The bitter earthy flavour of West Indian molasses is a wonderful complement to the sweet dates and sticky toffee. It can be prepared as one pudding or individual servings, and may be steamed in a traditional pudding steamer or in an open topped bowl, once there is a lid over the saucepan. A large covered saucepan with a pasta basket that can hold the large bowl works well for steamer.

1 cup 7oz/220g chopped, seedless dates
1 teaspoon baking soda (soda bicarbonate)
1/2 cup boiling water
1/4 cup rum
4oz/125g softened butter or margarine
1/3 cup 2oz/60g brown sugar
1/4 cup 2floz/60ml molasses/treacle
3 eggs
1/2 cup 4floz/125ml milk
1 2/3 cups 8 oz/250g flour
3 heaping teaspoons baking powder

(if using self-raising flour reduce baking powder to 1 teaspoon)
1/2 teaspoon salt

Toffee
1 cup 8floz/250ml golden syrup
1/2 cup 3oz/90g brown sugar
4oz/125g butter

To Serve (Optional)
2 small tubs whipping cream

1. Grease a 2 pint/1.2l pudding tin, globe tin or 10 individual serving pudding tins.
2. If the seedless dates are whole, process them for a couple of minutes in the food processor. Combine the dates, baking soda and boiling water and allow to stand for 15 minutes.
3. To make the toffee, put the golden syrup, brown sugar and butter into a small saucepan and bring to the boil. Reduce the heat to medium/low and simmer for 15-20 minutes. It should form a chewy ball when dropped in a saucer of cold water. Keep a close eye on it because it can burn quickly.
4. Remove the toffee from the heat and pour half of it into the container/s you are steaming the pudding/s in. Set aside the other half in the saucepan to reheat and serve with the pudding.
5. Put the steaming saucepan with water on to the heat and bring the water to the boil. A large saucepan with an inner basket such as those used for cooking

pasta, is ideal. If you are doing 10 individual puddings you will need 2 large steaming saucepans.
6. Place the butter, sugar, molasses, eggs, milk, flour, baking powder and salt into a food processor and process for 20 seconds (Do not over process). Add the date mixture and rum and process for 5 seconds.
7. Place the pudding mixture into the steaming bowl/s. Allow plenty of space in the bowl/s for the pudding to rise. Place in the saucepan, cover and steam the small puddings for 30-40 minutes or the large single pudding for 1 to 11/2 hours. The pudding is ready when an inserted skewer comes out clean.
8. Turn out and serve along with the rest of the toffee, reheated, (When left to stand the toffee may set hard but once reheated it will melt back into a sauce). Fresh whipped cream can also be served along with this pudding (To successfully whip cream in a warm

room, place the cream and the bowl in the freezer for 10 minutes before whipping).
9. This pudding can be made ahead of time and warmed up when you are ready to serve.

Serves 8-12

chocolate icebox pudding

The sponge cake called for in this recipe is the true sponge cake – that is, slightly lemon flavoured and made with no butter or shortening. Luckily, these are sold ready-made and are widely available at most supermarkets. If, however, you are unable to buy one but would still like to make this pudding, make a Victoria sponge using the cake recipe from the coconut cake on page 150 or a chocolate sponge from the chocolate cake recipe on page (148).

I store bought sponge cake (made without butter or shortening, if possible)
1/4 cup/4 tablespoons cream sherry
8oz/250g semi-sweet chocolate (bar or chocolate chips)
4 eggs
4 tablespoons whipping cream
4 tablespoons sugar

Garnish: I cup whipping cream and I small square of chocolate or semi sweet chocolate chips reserved from the bar used in the recipe

1. Slice up the sponge cake and divide in half. Put the first half in the bottom of a 10" dessert dish. Sprinkle with 1/8 cup of sherry. Set aside the rest of the sponge and sherry.
2. Melt chocolate in a double boiler, or in a covered bowl on a saucepan of boiling water, reserving a small square or a few chocolate chips for garnishing.
3. Separate the eggs, being extremely careful not to get any yolk in the whites. It is best to separate each egg into a little bowl, so that if you make a slip it doesn't affect all the egg whites. Place the egg whites into a very dry, clean, medium mixing bowl.
4. Place the yolks in a small mixing bowl along with the sugar and beat with an electric beater until creamy.
5. Take the melted chocolate off the heat and add the beaten egg yolk mixture and 4 tablespoons of cream.
6. Wash and dry the beater blades thoroughly. Beat the egg whites until as light and fluffy as possible, (about 5 minutes).

7. Fold the beaten egg whites into the chocolate mixture until well blended.
8. Scoop half of this on to the sherry soaked cake in the dish. Place the rest of the cake slices, sprinkle with sherry and top with the rest of the chocolate mixture.
9. Cover and refrigerate.
   A short while before serving, whisk the double cream until stiff and place on top of the pudding. The cream will whip most successfully if you chill the bowl with the cream in the freezer for about 10 minutes just before whisking. Sprinkle on the reserved chocolate chips or grate the reserved chocolate on top, using the large side of the grater.

Serves 8

baked custards, crème caramel & brulée

There are many variations to these custards. The baked custard can be an exotic ginger custard by adding a teaspoon fresh grated ginger to the custard and garnished with ground ginger when baked. The water in the creme caramel can be replaced with a can of unsweetened creme of coconut to make a delicious coconut creme caramel. Add a teaspoon of finely grated orange peel and replace the water with orange juice for an orange creme caramel. Guava stew can be placed in the bottom of the baked custard to creme brulée before pouring in the custard and baking.

Baked Custard

I tin 8floz/250ml condensed milk
I tin 8floz/250ml water
4 eggs
I teaspoon vanilla essence
I tablespoon butter
Garnish: Freshly grated nutmeg

1. Preheat the oven to 325F, 160C or Gas Mark 4
2. Place the condensed milk, water, eggs, vanilla essence and butter in a blender and blend for a minute.
3. Pour into a 8"/20cm diameter dish that is about 2"/5cm deep. Garnish with grated nutmeg.
4. Place in a pan of boiling water and place carefully in the oven. Bake for 35-40 minutes. It is ready when an inserted skewer comes out clean.

Serves 4-6

Crème Caramel

1/3 cup castor sugar
I tin 8floz/250ml condensed milk
I tin 8floz/250ml water
4 eggs
I teaspoon vanilla essence

1. Place the sugar in a stainless steel dish that you plan to bake the creme caramel in and place this on the stove, stirring often. When it starts to turn brown, stir vigourously until it all turns a deep golden brown. Plunge the pan into about 4"/10cm water to cool it quickly, turning it to make sure the caramel hardens evenly on the bottom. Set aside.
2. Place the condensed milk, water, eggs and vanilla essence in a blender and blend for a minute.
3. Pour into the dish that has the caramel.
4. Place the creme caramel dish into a saucepan with approx 2"/5cm boiling water that will hold the caramel custard pan. Cover the saucepan. Reduce the heat to very low and cook for 30-40 minutes. It is ready when an inserted skewer comes out clean. Cool and chill.
5. Keeps for 2-3 days in the fridge.
6. When ready to serve, turn it out into a shallow dish.

Serves 4-6

Crème Brulée

1/4 cup castor sugar for crème
2 cups 8floz/250ml double cream
4 eggs yolks
I teaspoon vanilla essence
I cup drained guava stew (optional)
1/3 cup castor sugar for brulée

1. Preheat a cool oven to 325F, 160C or Gas Mark 3
2. Gently warm the cream and vanilla essence in a small pan and set aside.
3. Whisk the egg yolks and sugar until creamy. Add the warm cream and mix.
4. If using, divide the guava stew into 4-6 portions. Slice and place the guavas in the bottoms of the 4-6 ramekin dishes and then pour in the crème.
5. Place in a baking pan with 1"/2/5cm of boiling water, and bake for 30-40 minutes. They are ready when an inserted skewer comes out clean. Set aside and cool.
6. When ready to serve, sprinkle with a tablespoon of sugar on each custard. Either place under the grill until the sugar turns golden brown and bubbles or turn the sugar to a crispy caramel using a hand held kitchen blow torch for that purpose.

Serves 4-6

chocolate fudge

This is a delicate recipe that must be followed to the letter in order to be successful. If you don't boil it long enough, or if you beat it too little, the fudge won't set. On the other hand, if you boil it too long, or beat it too much, it's likely to set in the saucepan or become too hot and thus set in unattractive crystalized lumps.

2 1/2 cups 1lb/500g light brown sugar
1/2 cup 4floz/125ml milk
6oz/185g butter
1 cup 3oz/90g cocoa
3 teaspoons vanilla essence

6"x10"/15cmx25cm pan buttered

1. Put the sugar and milk in a medium pan and bring to the boil.
2. Add the cocoa and butter and stir over a high heat until the butter has completely melted and the cocoa is blended in.
3. Reduce the heat to low and simmer without stirring, for 5-8 minutes. It is ready to beat when a drop of the mixture forms a soft ball in a saucer of cool water.
4. Remove from the heat and add the vanilla essence. Then tilt the pan and beat vigorously for about three minutes until the fudge gets quite thick but still pourable. Be careful not to beat the fudge for too long as it may set right there in the saucepan, if you beat it too little, however, it won't set at all and you'll end up with chocolate toffee. Also, be very careful not to splatter this mixture or spill it on yourself or anyone else - hot fudge can give a serious burn.
5. Pour into the buttered pan.
6. As it begins to set, (about 10 minutes) score with pointed knife into 1" squares. Completely sets in about 20 minutes.

7. Once set, turn it out with one firm knock upside down on to a wooden chopping board. Break into individual pieces along with the score lines.
8. Store in an airtight container or package in wax paper.

Variation:
Peanut Fudge
Follow the recipe for chocolate fudge, but substitute the cocoa with a cup 8floz/250ml of crunchy peanut butter. Keep the stove very low when simmering as this fudge tends to burn easily.

chocolate cake

As with all the cakes in this book, this is a quick-mix recipe that makes use of the ever-convenient food processor. The method of decoration, as pictured, is actually quite simple, and may look impressive even if mistakes are made.

Cake

1/3 cup 1 1/2 oz/45g cocoa
1/2 cup 4floz/125ml boiling water
6 oz/185g softened butter or margarine
1/2 cup 4 oz/125g granulated sugar
1/4 cup 2 oz/60g brown sugar
3 eggs
1/2 cup 4floz/124ml milk
2 teaspoons vanilla essence
1 cup 5oz/155g flour
1/2 teaspoon salt

3 heaping teaspoons baking powder (if using self raising flour reduce baking powder to 1 teaspoon)

Icing

2 cups 8oz/250g icing sugar
1/3 cup 1 1/2oz/45g cocoa
2oz/60g softened butter
1 teaspoon vanilla essence
1-2 tablespoons strong coffee
Small tube of white icing for decorating

Cake

1. Grease two 7"or 8"/17cmor20cm cake tins with butter or margarine. Cut out two circles of greaseproof paper and line each tin. Grease the surface of the paper and take a little of the cocoa to dust the greased tin.
2. Preheat a moderate oven 350F, 180C or Gas Mark 4.
3. Place the butter/margarine, sugars, eggs, (Break each egg into a small bowl before putting into the processor to check the freshness) milk, essence and cocoa paste into the food processor. Lastly, sift in the flour, baking powder and salt. Process for 20 seconds (Do not overprocess).
4. Spread cake mix evenly into the two pans. Bake in the centre of the oven for 20-25 minutes until risen and a skewer inserted into the middle comes out clean.
5. Turn out the cakes onto a wire rack to cool, removing the paper backing.

Icing

1. When the cakes are completely cool, sift the icing sugar and cocoa into a medium bowl and add the butter and vanilla essence. Add the hot coffee a bit at a time until the icing develops a good spreading consistency.
2. Place one cake on a plate, spread 1/2 the icing with a knife and repeat with the second cake on top. To make the spreading easier you can dip the knife into hot water or coffee.

To decorate

1. Squeeze a small ring of white icing around the centre, then a larger one around the first, continuing outwards until the last ring is about an inch from the edge of the cake. If you cannot get a tube of white icing, make a little white icing with icing sugar and water. Place it in a small plastic bag and snip a tiny hole in the bottom corner of the bag and proceed to squeeze the lines of icing to make the rings on the cake.

2. To feather the rings, drag the sharp point of a skewer or knife through the icing, from the centre of the cake out to the edge and then an inch further around drag the point of the skewer from the edge back into the centre, alternating around the cake.

coconut cake

Though extremely delicious, this cake does not keep very well and is therefore best eaten the same day.

6oz/185g softened butter or margarine
1 cup 6oz/185g straw or golden sugar
3 eggs
1/2 cup 4floz/125ml milk
1 teaspoon vanilla essence
1 teaspoon almond essence
1 1/4 cups 7oz/220g flour
3 heaping teaspoons baking powder (if using self-raising flour reduce baking powder to 1 teaspoon)
1/2 teaspoon salt

Icing
2 cups 8oz/250g icing sugar
2 tablespoons water
1 teaspoon almond essence
2 cups 12oz/375g fresh or frozen, finely grated coconut
Garnish: Cherries and angelica (optional)

1. Preheat a moderate oven 350F, 180C or Gas Mark 4.
2. Grease two 6"/15cm or 8"/20cm cake tins. Cut out a circle of greaseproof paper and line each tin, butter the surface of the paper and dust with flour.
3. Place all ingredients in the order that they are listed into a food processor, sifting in the flour, baking powder and salt (break each egg into a small bowl before putting into the processor to check the freshness).
4. Process for 25-35 seconds (Do not over process).
5. Spread cake mix evenly into the two pans.
6. Bake in the centre of the oven for 20-25 minutes until risen, golden brown and a skewer inserted into the centre comes out clean.
7. Turn out the cakes onto a wire rack to cool, removing the paper backing.
8. When the cakes are cool. Mix the icing sugar and almond essence and add the water gradually to make a spreading consistency.
9. Place one cake on a cake plate, spread 1/2 the icing on top, followed by 1/2 the coconut and repeat. Decorate with cherries (and angelica if you have it).

banana bread/coconut bread

Banana Bread: This nutritious Caribbean speciality is a great way to use up over-ripe bananas. It is deliciously moist so there is no temptation to spread it with butter.

Coconut Bread: This is a sweet, stodgy bread that goes well with an early morning mug or afternoon cup of tea. This recipe, prepared to yield a moist coconut bread, may be adjusted by halving the margarine and the lard to create a dryer loaf.

Banana Bread
1 1/2 cups 7oz/220g whole-wheat flour 1 tsp baking soda
1 tsp baking powder
1/2 tsp salt
1/3 cup 3floz/100ml oil
2/3 cup 6oz/185g brown sugar
2 eggs
6 medium bananas (very ripe is best)
2 tbsps molasses (optional)
Raisins & chopped nuts (optional)
1 tsp cinnamon
1 tsp nutmeg
1 tsp clove
1 tsp vanilla essence

1. Preheat oven to 350F, 180C or Gas Mark 3. Grease two medium loaf tins. Cut two strips of paper the lenght of the tins plus the height of the two ends plus two inches. Place along the tin with an inch protruding at each end, which you use to easily lift the cooked bread out of the tin.
2. Place all the ingredients in a food processor and process for 20 seconds (Do not over process). Finally, add raisins and chopped nuts, if desired and process for a further 5 seconds.
3. Place in the two loaf tins. Sprinkle with extra cinnamon and sugar.
4. Bake for 50 minutes or until an inserted skewer comes out clean. Lift out onto racks and allow to cool.

Coconut Bread
4oz/125g margarine
4oz/125g lard
1 tsp vanilla essence
1/2 cup 4oz/125g brown sugar
1 egg
1/4 cup 2floz/60ml water or coconut water
4oz/125g grated coconut
1 1/3 cups 8oz/250g flour
Dash cinnamon, mixed spice, nutmeg
1 teaspoon baking powder (heaping)
1/4 cup/3 tablespoons raisins (optional)
1/4 cup glac cherries (optional)

1. Preheat oven to 325F, 160C or Gas Mark 3. Grease two small loaf tins. Cut two strips of paper the lengthof the tins plus the height of theing.
3. Process for 20 seconds.
4. Add the raisins if you are including these and process for a further 5 seconds.
5. Place the mixture in the two loaf tins in equal amounts. Garnish with sugar, reserved grated coconut and cherries, if using.
6. Bake in the centre of the oven for about an hour or until an inserted skewer comes out clean. Lift out onto racks and allow to cool.

Garnish: Light brown sugar, grated coconut and cherries

date bread/ginger bread

Date Bread: This is a delicious, easy to make and a very healthy addition to teatime or mid-morning coffee. It is especially delicious when spread with a little butter.

Ginger Bread: This delicious old fashioned recipe uses the very easy melting method.

Date Bread
1 cup 7oz/220g stoned and chopped dates
1 teaspoon baking soda
3/4 cup 6floz/190ml boiling water
1 tablespoon butter
3/4 cup 4oz/125g sugar
1 egg
1 3/4 cups 9oz/280g flour
1 teaspoon baking powder
Pinch salt

1. If the seedless dates are whole, chop them in the food processor. This is noisy, but effective. Mix the dates, baking soda and boiling water and allow to cool.
2. Heat the oven to 325F, 160C or Gas Mark 3.
3. Grease a 4 x 8 /10cmx20cm loaf tin. Cut a piece of wax paper the sum length of the bottom and two ends of the tin plus 2 /5cm. Line the loaf tin with wax paper sticking up at either end, which will be used to easily lift the cooked bread out of the tin. Grease this and dust the pan with a little flour.
4. Place the butter, sugar, egg and date mixture in a food processor. Sift the flour, baking powder and salt into the food processor. Process for 20 seconds (Do not over process).
5. Pour into the loaf tin and bake for about an hour or until an inserted skewer comes out clean.
6. Lift out and cool on a rack.

Ginger Bread
1/2 cup 3oz/90g sugar
2oz/60g butter
2oz/6-g lard
1/2 cup 4floz/125ml golden syrup
1/2 cup 4floz/125ml molasses/treacle (use a full cup of golden syrup, if you re not using molasses/treacle)
1/4 cup water
1/2 teaspoon ground clove
1/2 teaspoon salt
1 teaspoon ground cinammon
1/4 cup/4 tablespoons ground ginger
2 1/2 cups 14oz/440g flour
1 egg
1 1/2 teaspoons baking soda

1. Preheat the oven to 325F, 160C or Gas Mark 3.
2. Grease a 10 /25cm square pan or equivalent. Cut a piece of wax paper the sum width of the bottom and two sides of the tin plus 2 /5cm. Line the tin with wax paper sticking up at either side, which will be used to easily lift the cooked bread out of the tin. Grease this and dust the pan with a little flour.
3. Melt the butter, syrup, water and sugar in a medium saucepan.
4. Sift the dry ingredients into a medium mixing bowl.
5. Whisk an egg and add to the dry ingredients along with the melted ingredients and mix well.
6. Bake for about 45 minutes or until a skewer comes out clean.
7. Turn out and cool on a wire rack.
8. Cut into squares.

marble cake

This is a good cake for children's parties or just to make with children for the fun of it. The icing is especially funky and quite easy to do. You can let your creativity flow and decorate with little coloured sweets or candy such as smarties, fruit jellies and wine gums. Another possibility is to bake it in two small loaf tins and make an enchanted house, cutting the second loaf into the shape of a roof and covering it with candies. The orange rind and juice in the icing tends give the whole cake a delicious orange flavour.

6oz/185g softened butter or margarine
3/4 cup 6oz/185g granulated sugar
3 eggs
1/2 cup 4floz/125ml milk
1 teaspoon vanilla essence
1 cup 6oz/185g flour
3 heaping teaspoons baking powder (if using self raising flour reduce baking powder to 1 teaspoon)
1/2 teaspoon salt
Red, blue, yellow and green food dye

Icing
2 cups12oz/375g icing sugar
2-3 tablespoons freshly squeezed orange juice
1 teaspoon finely grated orange rind
Red, blue, yellow and green food dye
Garnish: sprinkles, jellies, smarties etc

1. Preheat a moderate oven 350F,180C or Gas Mark 4.
2. Grease two 7"/18cm or 8"/20cm cake tins, cut out a circle of greaseproof paper and line each tin, butter the surface of the paper and dust with flour.
3. Place all ingredients except the food dyes, in the order that they are listed into a food processor, sifting in the flour, baking powder and salt. (break each egg into a small bowl before putting into the processor to varify their freshness). Process for 20 seconds (Do not over process).
4. To dye the cake mix into four different colours, place three quarters of the cake mix in three small bowl leaving the fourth quarter of cake mix in the processor. Squirt a couple of drops of each colour food dye into each bowl and the food processor and mix in, stirring as little as possible. You can mix the one in the food processor by processing for a second. Place 1/2 of each colour in each baking pan and spread.
5. Bake in the centre of the oven for approx 20 minutes until risen, golden brown and a skewer inserted into the centre comes out clean.
6. Turn out the cakes onto a wire rack to cool, removing the paper backing.
7. Sift the icing sugar, add the orange rind and gradually add the orange juice to make a spreading consistency.
8. Divide the icing into four separate little bowls. You can leave a quarter in the original bowl and squirt two drops of each colour dye into each bowl and mix well.
9. Place one cake on a cake plate, place 1/2 of each colour icing strategically on each quarter of the cake. Spread the icing in a circular motion in the same direction so that each colour runs into the next. Repeat on the top and decorate. This recipe gives enough icing to ice the sides of the cake so if you prefer to ice only the top and middle (for simplicity) you can use 8oz icing sugar and 1 1/2 tablespoons of orange juice.

cookies

Coconut Oat Cookies and Peanut Cookies: Store away these nutritious cookies in an airtight container as soon as they are cool since they tend to go soft easily. They freeze very well.

Orange Refrigerator Cookies: The rolled, raw cookie mixture can then be stored in the freezer for months, ready to bake on demand.

Coconut Oat Cookies

8oz/250g margarine
1 cup 6oz/185g sugar
3/4 cup 4oz/125g brown sugar
2 eggs
1 1/2 teaspoons vanilla essence
1/4 teaspoon salt
2 cups 10oz/315g flour
1 1/2 tsp baking soda
1 teaspoon baking powder
2 cups rolled oats
2 cups 5oz/155g corn flakes
3/4 cup 4oz/125g grated coconut
1/2 cup 2oz/60g sunflower seeds

1. Preheat oven to 350F, 180C or Gas Mark 4.
2. Place the margarine, sugar, eggs, vanilla essence, sifted flour, baking soda, salt, oats and coconut in a food processor. Process for 20 seconds (Do not over process).
3. Add cornflakes and sunflower seeds and process for a further 10 seconds.
4. Drop teaspoonfuls on ungreased baking sheets and flatten. Bake for 14-16 minutes or until golden.
5. Cool on racks.

Makes 50-60 cookies

Peanut Cookies

4oz/125g margarine
1 cup 8oz/250g peanut butter
1 cup 6oz/185g sugar
3/4 cup brown sugar
2 eggs
1 1/2 teaspoons vanilla
1/4 teaspoon salt
2 cups 10oz/315g flour
1 1/2 teaspoons baking soda
(bicarbonate of soda)
1 teaspoon baking powder
2 cups 5oz/155g rolled oats
2 cups 8oz/250g unsalted roasted peanuts

1. Preheat oven to 325F, 160C or Gas Mark 3.
2. Place all the ingredients in a food processor and process for 25 seconds (Do not over process). Reserve a few peanuts for decorating.
3. Drop teaspoonfuls and flatten, on an ungreased baking sheet and decorate with a peanut in the centre.
4. Bake for 10-15 minutes or until golden. Watch these cookies carefully as they tend to burn easily.
5. Cool on racks.

Makes 40-50 cookies

Orange Refrigerator Cookies

1 cup 6oz/185g sugar (granulated or light brown crystal)
4oz/125g softened butter
1 egg
1 teaspoon vanilla
1 teaspoon grated orange rind
1 1/2 cups 9oz/280g sifted flour
1/2 teaspoon salt
1 1/2 teaspoons baking powder
Garnish: white sugar

1. Place all the ingredients into a food processor for 20-30 seconds.
2. On a floured surface roll the cookie dough into a solid cylinder shaped roll.
3. Wrap with waxed paper, twisting two ends tightly. Freeze for 2 hours or until you require the cookies. They will last in a freezer for months.
4. When you are ready to bake the cookies, preheat the oven at 400F, 200C or Gas Mark 6.
5. Butter a cookie sheet.
6. Unwrap the cookie roll. Slice with a sharp knife. Shape and decorate as you wish and sprinkle with sugar.
7. Place on the cookie sheet and bake for 10-12 minutes or until light golden.

Makes about 40 small cookies

small dinner parties

Small Dinner Parties Preparing dinner for 4-6 people gives you the opportunity to make guests feel truly cherished. You can luxuriate in attending to details, especially if you do preparation the day before. These menues are geared to simple dining where all three courses can be enjoyed.

Menu 1

Pork wontons

Chicken creole
Black beans and rice
Plantain wrapped in bacon
Green beans and almonds

Lime meringue pie

Menu 2

Sesame chicken wings

Barbequed fish
Breadfruit in butter sauce
Okra creole
Green beans and almonds

Chocolate icebox pudding

Menu 3

Crab crepe

Glazed ham with hot sorrel sauce
Pigeon peas and rice
Pumpkin fritters
Christophene au gratin

Mango mousse with passion fruit sauce

Menu 4

Pumpkin soup

Blackened fish and salad with white rice or fresh tuna salad

Sticky toffee pudding served with caramel sauce and whipped cream

Menu 5

Rum chicken liver pate and salad served with melba toast and mango chutney

Chilli shrimp
White steamed rice

Sticky pineapple upside down

Menu 6

Avocado, paw paw and shrimp salad

Stew down pork chops
Sweet potato balls
Mixed vegetables in cheese sauce

Lime cheesecake

Cold buffets are ideal when a family or large group are gathering and you don't want to be stuck in the kitchen during the party. For all buffets, try and make as much as possible the day before, so you can enjoy your own party. Best of all, have a bring along party and get each group to bring one of the dishes.

Buffet Lunch

Ti panche
Bentley

Ackee and salt fish or
Soused conch served with crackers

Roast pork, with crackling and gravy
Fried fish
Sweet potato balls
Pigeon peas and rice
Pumpkin fritters
Christophene au gratin

Chocolate cake served with ice cream
Mango mousse and passion fruit sauce

Buffet Dinner

Passiontinis

Fish terrine with mango salsa served with melba toast

Baked leg of ham with hot sorrel sauce
Fish in white sauce
Orange sweet potato bake
Black eye peas and rice
Seven layer salad
Corn pie
Eggplant fritters

Lime meringue pie
Chocolate icebox pudding

Cold Buffet - Cold buffet - also suitable for picnics and boat trips

Rum punch
Punch a creme
Lemonade

Buljol and crackers

Cold shrimp with marie rose sauce
Pasta salad
Pickled breadfruit
Soused pork chops
Steamed pudding
Sesame chicken wings
Macaroni cheese
Potato salad
Seven layer salad

Ginger bread
Coconut bread
Fudge

everyday meals

Menu 1

Pumpkin soup
Fresh tuna salad

Menu 4

Calallou
Chicken pelau

Menu 7

Blackened fish
White steamed rice
Salad

Menu 10

Fried fish
Breadfruit or yam in butter sauce
Dressed cucumber

Menu 2

Split pea soup
Chicken chow mein

Menu 5

Big soup

Menu 8

Kedgeree
Tomato basil salad
Mixed green salad with
Caribbean french dressing

Menu 11

Chicken creole
Steamed rice
Eggplant fritters
Green beans

Menu 3

Gazpacho
Chicken Pelau

Menu 6

Salt fish and cou cou
Dressed cucumber

Menu 9

Stewed down pork chops
Yam or sweet potato pie
Christophene au gratin
Pumpkin fritters

Menu 9

Chicken curry and rice
Pumpkin
Onion and sweet pepper with natural
yogurt
Eggplant choka
Tomato
Cumumber

Small Tea Party

Cucumber sandwiches

Cheese and crackers
with Mango chutney

Peanut cookies

Sticky toffee pudding

Large Tea Party

Cucumber sandwiches
Cheese sandwiches

Fish terrine with melba toast

Ginger bread

Chocolate cake

Coconut oat cookies

Childrens Party

Bentley and lemondade

Fish cakes

Chicken wings

Orange refrigerator cookies

Fudge

Marble cake

index